PROCOPIUS

BY

J.A.S. EVANS

The chief aim of this book is to introduce the general reader to Procopius of Caesarea, the greatest historian of the age of Justinian. Procopius enters the pages of history in 527, the year that Justinian himself became emperor. In that year, Procopius became legal advisor and secretary to the general Belisarius, whose splendid military career was to take him from the eastern frontiers of the empire, to North Africa, Italy, and back again to the East. Procopius was to accompany him almost continuously until 540 A.D., and perhaps even later.

His most important work was his *History of the Wars of Justinian,* of which the first seven books were published in 551, and the last book added sometime later. But the work which has done the most to make Procopius known to the general reader, is one which can never have been published during his lifetime. Called the *Anekdota* or more commonly, the *Secret History,* it presents a malevolent view of Justinian's reign.

Professor Evans deals with the main questions about Procopius in this book: when he wrote his works, what his religious outlook was, and most important, why he wrote his bitter *Secret History,* and for whom. Procopius emerges as a member of the ruling *élite* of the late Empire, whose position was threatened by Justinian's innovations. He came to regard the emperor and his wife Theodora as arch—demons. The *Secret History* was written in the first instance for Procopius' own satisfaction, but it fell into the hands of some trusted and like-minded executors, who handed it on to posterity.

TWAYNE'S WORLD AUTHORS SERIES (TWAS)

The purpose of TWAS is to survey the major writers —novelists, dramatists, historians, poets, philosophers, and critics—of the nations of the world. Among the national literatures covered are those of Australia, Canada, China, Eastern Europe, France, Germany, Greece, Italy, Japan, Latin America, New Zealand, Poland, Russia, Scandinavia, Spain, and the African nations, as well as Hebrew, Yiddish, and Latin Classical literature. This survey is complemented by Twayne's United States Authors Series and English Authors Series.

The intent of each volume in these series is to present a critical-analytical study of the works of the writer; to include biographical and historical material that may be necessary for understanding, appreciation, and critical appraisal of the writer; and to present all material in clear, concise English—but not to vitiate the scholarly content of the work by doing so.

Procopius

By J. A. S. EVANS

McMaster University
Hamilton, Canada

Twayne Publishers, Inc.   ::   New York

Preface

Among English-speaking scholars, Procopius has received a curious mixture of neglect and attention. He has been widely read, though often at secondhand, through historical novels and dramas whose authors have pillaged him freely for material. Historians have been grateful to him because he is the most important single source for the reign of Justinian, which is one of the pivotal periods in the history of the world. Edward Gibbon's reliance on him must impress anyone who reads the relevant chapters in *The Decline and Fall of the Roman Empire;* at one point, he inserted the tribute: "For the troubles of Africa, I neither have nor desire another guide than Procopius, whose eye contemplated the image and whose ear collected the reports of the innumerable events of his own times." We may imagine that Gibbon admired Procopius in part because he had prejudices which had something in common with those of Procopius but for a modern opinion, we can turn to Percy Neville Ure's *Justinian and His Age,* one of the best compact histories of the period. Ure, who examined the achievements of Justinian through the eyes of his contemporaries as far as possible, gives equally generous attention to Procopius.

Yet there has been relatively little serious study of his merits as a historian. This is the first book written in English on Procopius, although the Germans have done better, and we can thank nineteenth-century scholars such as W. Teuffel, Felix Dahn, and later, Jacob Haury, for putting Procopian scholarship on a firm basis. The neglect in the English-speaking world has been mainly due to two circumstances. First, Gibbon's thesis that Constantinople was in a state of decay for a thousand years is a trifle farfetched if we think about it, but nevertheless it became the conventional wisdom of the nineteenth century, and only in the last generation or so has Byzantium received greater, and less prejudiced, attention. Second, Procopius belongs to a period which classical historians regard as beyond their own home ground, and which medievalists have tended to neglect in favor of western Europe. He is a historian who is often referred to, and seldom studied.

I have aimed in this book to present a general study of Procopius rather than a scholarly work. The first chapter deals with the historian's background and with his life as far as we know anything about it. I have avoided a surfeit of conjectures: we know that he came from Caesarea in Palestine and that he was aristocratic in his outlook, well educated, and rather snobbish about it. Beyond this we can proceed with inferences from his works, many of them sound, but our certain information peters out before long.

The next three chapters deal with his writings: the *History of the Wars,* which was his major achievement, the panegyric on Justinian's building program, and the *Secret History* or *Anekdota,* which is one of the strangest survivals that we have from the ancient world. I have accepted the general view that the *Secret History* was written by Procopius without going into the arguments. Those scholars who have doubted that Procopius was the author have generally proposed as an alternative that it was written by an anonymous contemporary who posed as Procopius, which is rather like the venerable thesis about Homer: that the *Iliad* was not written by Homer but by someone else of the same name who lived at the same time.

Then follows a chapter where I have tried to document from internal evidence in the *Wars,* how Procopius' attitude changed from one of relative optimism and acceptance of Justinian's regime in 527, when he started his career as Belisarius' secretary, to the bitter hostility of the *Secret History.* I conclude that Procopius accepted the conventional concepts of the empire as an imitation of heaven and the emperor as the viceregent of God; and when he saw the empire afflicted with an emperor (and empress) who offended his conservative principles and lightened the purses of his own social class with their reforms and innovations on the one hand, and with natural catastrophes such as plagues, earthquakes, and floods on the other, he could not find an explanation except by recalling the prophecies of the Antichrist and by making Justinian into the prince of the devils endowed with supernatural power to create havoc. Next, I examine Procopius' historical outlook and conclude that, for all his apparent use of pagan concepts in the *Wars,* he was an orthodox Christian, a participant in the thought world of the late Roman Empire, whose views can find parallels in Saint Augustine and Boethius. Finally, the epilogue attempts to gather up the strands and briefly to trace Procopius' later influence.

It remains for me to thank those who have assisted me with this small book: McMaster University and the chairman of the department of history, Dr. G. S. French, for granting me a half-year leave of absence in which to complete it, the Canada Council for a research grant, and the University of Victoria for the use of its library during one productive summer. Professor T. F. Carney of the University of Manitoba has given me many useful comments on Procopius' attitudes and his traditionalist outlook. By no means least, I owe a debt of thanks to my wife for her help in preparing the manuscript, and to Mary Gianos, the editor of this series, for encouraging me to undertake this study.

Contents

Chronology

474– 491	Reign of the emperor Zeno in the eastern Roman Empire.
476	Romulus Augustulus, last emperor of the western empire, was deposed by Odovacar, who ruled Italy himself for the next seventeen years, nominally as a subordinate of the emperor Zeno.
489– 493	Invasion of Italy by the Ostrogoths, led by Theodoric the Amal. Odovacar captured and murdered.
ca. 482	Justinian born, as Flavius Petrus Sabbatius, at Taurisium in the Illyrian province, Dacia Mediterranea.
491– 518	Reign of the emperor Anastasius.
ca. 500	Birth of the historian Procopius at Caesarea in Palestine.
518– 527	Reign of Justinian's uncle, Justin I.
524	King Cabades I of Persia opened war on the empire, driving the Romans out of Caucasian Iberia (Georgia).
525	Justin made Justinian Caesar, marking him as his successor.
526	(Aug. 30). Theodoric died in Italy, leaving the throne to his grandson Atalaric, under the regency of his mother, Amalasuntha.
527	(April 4). Justinian made co-emperor with Justin; by this time he had already married Theodora. (August 1). Death of Justin, leaving Justinian sole emperor. Also in this year, Belisarius was appointed commander of the troops at Daras on the Persian frontier, and Procopius became his legal secretary.
530	(June). Belisarius, who had been appointed General of the East, defeated the Persians at Daras.
531	(April). Belisarius defeated at Callinicum, after which he and Procopius returned to Constantinople. (September). Death of Cabades, who was succeeded by Chosroes.
532	(January). The "Nika" revolt broke out in Constantinople, nearly toppling Justinian's regime. It was crushed by Belisarius and Mundus, who massacred the rioters in the Hip-

podrome. In the spring of this year, the so-called Endless Peace was signed with Persia.

533 Belisarius, accompanied by Procopius, set out on the Vandal expedition.

534 The expedition came to a successful conclusion with the surrender, in March, of the Vandal king Gelimer, who was taken captive to Constantinople. Belisarius returned for a triumph, leaving Procopius in Libya. The Moorish revolt started. In Italy, Atalaric died (October 2), and Amalasuntha married her cousin, Theodatus, in order to retain power.

535 Theodatus imprisoned Amalasuntha in a coup; she was murdered in April while negotiations with Justinian were being carried on. Justinian prepared for war. Belisarius sent with small force against Ostrogothic Sicily. The island was surprised, and Syracuse was taken in December.

536 Mutiny among the Byzantine troops in Libya, led by Stotzas. The Byzantine commander in Libya, Solomon, and Procopius escaped to join Belisarius, who intervened without success. Later, Belisarius, now accompanied again by Procopius, invaded Italy, took Naples in the autumn, and entered Rome before the end of the year.

537 The mutiny in Libya was finally suppressed by Germanus. In Italy, Wittigis, who had replaced Theodatus as Gothic king the previous year, began his siege of Rome, which was defended brilliantly by Belisarius. In Constantinople, the church of Hagia Sophia was completed and dedicated (December 26).

538 Wittigis abandoned siege of Rome, and instead besieged John, the nephew of Vitalian in Ariminum. Dissension in the imperial command in Italy.

540 Belisarius received the surrender of the Goths, having tricked them into believing that he would declare himself independent king in Italy. After occupying Ravenna, he returned to Constantinople with Procopius. In the same year, Chosroes of Persia broke the "Endless Peace," invaded Syria, sacked Antioch, and attacked other cities.

541 Chosroes invaded Roman Lazica on the Black Sea and took the fortress of Petra. Belisarius, in command of the

Byzantine forces in Mesopotamia, advanced as far as Sisauranon, and then fell back. In Italy, Totila became new Ostrogothic king and rallied the Goths against the disorganized Byzantine forces. Bubonic plague broke out in Egypt and spread to Palestine.

542   The plague reached Constantinople, where Procopius witnessed it. On the Persian front, Chosroes threatened Palestine, but was halted by Belisarius, who was recalled shortly thereafter.

543   Totila overran much of Italy, taking Naples in the spring. Belisarius was under suspicion of disloyalty and his movements restricted.

544–   Belisarius returned to command in Italy, but he accom-
548   plished little.

545   Justinian made a five-year armistice with Persia.

548   (June 28). Death of the empress Theodora.

550   The emperor's cousin, Germanus, was named to command Byzantine forces in Italy, and collected an army, but died before he reached Italy. Narses was appointed Germanus' successor and began his preparations.

551   Procopius published the first seven books of the *History of the Wars*.

552   Narses defeated the Ostrogoths at Busta Gallorum, and Totila lost his life. His successor, Teias, was defeated by Narses at Mons Lactarius, near Mount Vesuvius. Also in this year, Justinian made a second five-year armistice with Persia.

557(?)   Procopius published the eighth book of his *Wars*, covering events to 552.

558   (May 7). The dome of Hagia Sophia partially collapsed.

558–   Procopius at work on his panegyric of Justinian's building
560   program. At the same time, he was probably at work on his *Secret History*, which began as a commentary on the first seven books of his *Wars*, and included material which it was unsafe to publish there.

561(?)   Death of Procopius.

562   The rebuilt church of Hagia Sophia was dedicated.

565   (March). The death of Belisarius. (November). The death of Justinian, who was succeeded by his nephew, Justin II.

CHAPTER 1

The Life and Times of Procopius

From his elevation to his death, Justinian governed the Roman empire thirty-eight years, seven months and thirteen days. The events of his reign, which excite our curious attention by their number, variety and importance, are diligently related by the secretary of Belisarius, a rhetorician whom eloquence had promoted to the rank of senator and prefect of Constantinople. According to the vicissitudes of courage or servitude, of favor or disgrace, Procopius successively composed the *history*, the *panegyric*, and the *satire* of his own times. The eight books of the Persian, Vandalic and Gothic wars . . . deserve our esteem as a laborious and successful imitation of the Attic, or at least of the Asiatic, writers of ancient Greece. His facts are collected from the personal experience and free conversation of a soldier, a statesman, and a traveller; his style continually aspires, and often attains to the merit of strength and elegance. . . .[1]

So WROTE Edward Gibbon, and his orotund prose is worth quoting, although we may quibble at details. For instance, it is doubtful if Procopius ever became prefect of Constantinople: a Procopius is listed as prefect for 562, but the name was not uncommon, and there is no good reason to think that this man was the historian. Yet Procopius, our chief source for the reign of Justinian, did possess one prime prerequisite for a great historian of the ancient world: he occupied a post with an excellent view of what went on. He appears first in history the year that Justinian ascended the throne, 527, when he became legal secretary to Belisarius, the greatest general of the age, and for the next fifteen years or so he followed him from Syria to North Africa and to Italy, taking part in the series of military campaigns which Justinian launched in his endeavor to restore the Roman Empire. He makes his exit about 560, or shortly after, when, interrupted perhaps by death, he ceased writing his last work, an

15

encomium on Justinian's building program throughout the empire, which he appears to have undertaken at the emperor's request, or rather, at his command. We may believe that by then Procopius was already well known for his *History of the Wars of Justinian,* which related in succession the campaigns on the eastern frontier against the Persian Empire, in Africa against the Vandals, and in Italy against the Ostrogoths. The first seven books appeared in 551, followed by an eighth book a few years later, which brought the story down to the final victory over the Goths in Italy in 552. Then Procopius broke off. It was not for lack of wars to recount after 552, but rather, we may suspect, that accurate reporting of them would bring little credit to Justinian's regime, and might even involve the reporter in some personal danger. Procopius was to have a continuator, Agathias of Myrrhina, who carried on the *History of the Wars* from where Procopius left it, but he wrote after Justinian was dead.

Then comes Procopius' last published work, the *De Aedificiis* which we simply label the *Buildings*—the "panegyric . . . of his own time," as Gibbon called it. It is a cool panegyric, full of formal praise, and it was never finished.[2] However, it demonstrates that Procopius was still on good terms with the aging emperor, who commissioned this exercise in public relations, and even gave some advice on the form he wished it to take.[3] Yet the real feelings which Procopius harbored about Justinian were very different, and these he entrusted to an unpublished essay, Gibbon's "satire of his own times," which usually goes now by the title of the *Secret History.* It is a slashing attack on the regime which devotes most of its venom to Justinian and Theodora, but it also includes Procopius' old commander Belisarius and his wife Antonina in the general condemnation.

How the *Secret History* survived is unknown. Had its existence come to the ears of the secret police while Justinian lived, it might well have meant imprisonment or even death for Procopius. But somehow it enjoyed an underground existence until it was safe for it to exist openly, and in the early seventeenth century a copy of it turned up in the Vatican Library. It has since become the most famous of Procopius' works and the most read, a fact which is less than fair both to the historian and to the emperor whom he lampooned.

About Procopius himself we know very little beyond what information we can glean from his own writings. The tidbit which Gibbon reproduces, that he was "promoted to the rank of senator," whether by his own eloquence or not, comes from a tenth-century lexicon called the *Souda,* which assigns him the rank of *illustris,* the only senatorial rank which actually possessed the right to speak in the Senate. We may be certain that he was a member of the traditional elite of the late empire, who had been well educated in the Greek classics and Roman law, and who took up a career in the imperial bureaucracy. He came from Herod the Great's old capital in Palestine, Caesarea, a fact which has led to some speculation about his racial origins. However, no matter what his blood lines were, he was a product of Greek culture and tradition, and he mentions with some disdain that Justinian, whose native tongue was Latin, never spoke Greek well. Yet at the beginning of his career Procopius must have been a promising young man, and if he was unenthusiastic about Justinian's policies, his views were well concealed. Otherwise he would hardly have been appointed to a position of trust as secretary of Belisarius. But as the wars of Justinian dragged on, whatever optimism Procopius had once had, turned to disillusion, and the tone of his *History of the Wars* becomes more critical. At times, the criticism touches the emperor himself, although, when it does, Procopius is generally prudent, and often veils his unflattering remark behind an artistic device. For instance, one of the traditions which Procopius had inherited from the classical Greek historians was the practice of composing speeches and putting them in the mouths of historical figures, and Procopius found this a useful practice. One would expect an enemy of the state to voice hostile sentiments. Thus, a renegade could describe Justinian as a man "who always sits unguarded in some lobby to a late hour of night, eagerly unrolling the Christian scriptures in company with priests who are at the extremity of old age."[4] Envoys sent by the Goths to Persia could delineate Justinian's character in terms which are emphasized again and again in the *Secret History* as Procopius' own sentiments: "For he is by nature an innovator, and he covets those things which absolutely do not belong to him, and he cannot abide by the established order. Therefore he desires to acquire the whole world, and his eagerness to seize every kingdom consumes him."[5] Finally, in the eighth book, written after the first seven books were published, Procopius barely takes pains to conceal his criticism.

The reign of Justinian was a period of change, as rapid, perhaps, as in the twentieth century. The Roman world ends with Justinian, and the Byzantine world begins. When Procopius accuses Justinian of innovation, he betrays the feelings of his own social stratum in the empire, which saw its position threatened by the changes of this transitional period, and regarded them with revulsion.

Not that Justinian ever intended to be a transitional figure. His aim was rather to renew and revitalize the Roman Empire, which meant that the lost provinces of the West had to be reconquered as far as was possible. For close to three centuries the Balkans had produced a remarkable series of Roman emperors who had saved the empire after the near-collapse in the third century and had carried it on during much of the fourth. Justinian was the last of a distinguished line. But first we should look at the background of the age which produced Justinian.

I *The Background*

If one asks a historian when the Roman Empire fell in the West, the date he will probably give is A.D. 476. Like a surprising number of dates in history, it is a date of convenience. In 476, the last Roman emperor in Italy, Romulus Augustulus, was deposed, and in view of his youth, was pensioned off rather than executed. At the time, there existed in Dalmatia another emperor of the West, whose claims were more legitimate than those of Romulus, but he died shortly after Romulus' deposition without contriving to upset the course of history, and even though 476 is only a convenient date, it is important for western Europe. Nothing stopped or started then, but empires live by symbols as much as by hard facts. When the warlord Odovacer, who deposed Romulus, sent the imperial insignia to Constantinople with a message to the emperor Zeno that henceforth the empire could manage with only one emperor, the idea of a single Roman world embracing the Mediterranean faded a trifle, but perceptibly, in the West.

For the East, 476 meant nothing. The eastern empire had been a separate entity administratively since the beginning of the century. This split was not what Constantine the Great had intended when he founded his new Rome on the shores of the Bosporus in 330 and named it after himself, Constantinople. The empire was one, and the concept of a united empire was to be maintained in the face of the facts for some centuries yet. It was to provide the mystique for Justinian's *renovatio* which was to take Byzantine armies as far west as Spain on expensive campaigns which the imperial treasury could ill afford. But actually, the two halves had been separated more than once after Constantine's death; and when Theodosius the Great died in 395, leaving his sons Arcadius and Honorius an inheritance divided into two empires, the separation became definitive. The empire of the East became a separate unit.

The formative years of the eastern empire were between 330 and 518. During this period, it managed to survive the barbarian invasions, although it was a narrow escape. At the end of the fourth century, the Visigoths were virtually in control of Constantinople, but their restlessness saved the empire. Alaric, the Visigothic leader, and his horde moved off to Italy and in 410 sacked Rome. Thirty years later, the Huns led by Attila threatened Constantinople, which survived more by good luck than by good management. When the Hun empire broke up after Attila died in 453, it was the turn of the Ostrogoths. The emperor Zeno (474-91) contrived to avert this danger by proposing to the Ostrogothic king Theodoric that he take Italy, which had reverted to Zeno's suzerainty after the deposition of Romulus Augustulus in 476, though the actual ruler of Italy was Odovacer. This suggestion was a shrewd move which accomplished two objectives: it punished Odovacer, who was an insubordinate vassal, or so Zeno considered him; and it rid the eastern empire of the menacing presence of the Ostrogoths. Theodoric ruled Italy well after he had disposed of Odovacer. Procopius' judgment of him is that he was 'in name a tyrant, but in fact a true king.'[6] Although he and his Goths were Arians, Theodoric managed to maintain generally good relations with the orthodox Catholics in his kingdom until just before his death.

The empire was a Christian one. Not that there were no pagans; when Constantine embraced Christianity in 311, it was still a minority religion with many competitors. No matter. With one exception only, all the emperors after Constantine were Christians, and with imperial favor, and its own impressive organization behind it, the church gained ground rapidly. At first the pagans were allowed freedom of worship. In the fourth century paganism even staged an intellectual revival, but it was not to last. The reign of Theodosius the Great (379-95) marks the turning point. Henceforth, the empire became an orthodox Christian state, and legal toleration of the pagans was at an end. Paganism by no means ceased to exist; in fact, the University of Athens, whose traditions went back to Plato and Aristotle, remained a pagan stronghold until Justinian closed it down in 529.

In the pages of Procopius, the pagans were given the label "Hellenes," which the classical Greeks had applied to themselves, and in his *Secret History* Procopius says that Justinian persecuted them cruelly.[7] In the history of paganism, as in a great many other things, Justinian marks the end of an era. However, the official view of Justinian's muscular missionary activity, which we get in the *Buildings,* was that it was the emperor's duty to promote the orthodox faith, forcibly if necessary. The *Buildings* notes with approbation that polytheism was ended at Awjila (Augila), far off in the interior of Libya, that Moors at Ghadames voluntarily went over to the Christian faith, and a tribe which lived close by Leptis Magna in North Africa was delivered from a "Hellenic" form of atheism.[8] The propagation of correct belief was one of the missions of a Byzantine emperor which Justinian took seriously.

But what was correct belief? This was a political issue as well as a question of theology; the two were inseparable and no one imagined that it could be otherwise. There were three great heresies which agitated the empire in the fourth and fifth centuries, all centering on the nature of the Trinity. The Greek East took theology seriously, and the nature of the Father and the Son could be discussed in the shops and the marketplace as freely then as hockey or football scores are today. Yet there was behind these disputes not merely a genuine concern for orthodoxy, but also the ambitions of the rival ecclesiastical sees of Rome, Alexandria, and Constantinople, and the incipient nationalism of Egypt and Syria.[9] Arianism, which denied that the Father and the Son could be of the same essence, was repudiated at the Council of Constantinople in 381; after that, it remained only a faith for the German barbarians, who had been reached first by Arian missionaries. The Ostrogoths in Italy and the Vandals in Libya were Arians, and with both of these, their religion tended to keep them segregated from the Catholic population which they had subjected. The second great heresy was Nestorianism, which insisted on the humanity of Christ. It was condemned in 431.

The third was Monophysitism, which taught that there was one nature in Christ, and it was divine. Monophysitism captured the allegiance of Egypt and Syria, split the empire, and embittered relations between the eastern provinces and Constantinople on the one hand, and between Rome and the emperor on the other. Zeno attempted a compromise to satisfy the Monophysites. It failed to win them over, but it did succeed in antagonizing the pope. Anastasius (485-518) was a Monophysite himself, and in the last years of his reign, he moved imperial policy as far as he dared toward the Monophysite camp. With Anastasius' successor Justin, the pendulum swung in the opposite direction. Justinian was orthodox, but his wife Theodora favored the Monophysites, and it was thanks partly to her protection that a Monophysite hierarchy developed during her husband's reign. By the time Justinian died, an organized Monophysite church was an accomplished fact in Syria and Egypt.

Imperial tradition, Greek culture, and Christian orthodoxy: these were the directing forces of Byzantine government and religion. The imperial tradition was inherited from Rome; the language of law and of the imperial bureaucracy was Latin, and in the schools of the East,[10] the aspiring sons of the empire's traditional elite cut their teeth on Virgil. Here, too, the reign of Justinian marks a change; most of his new laws after A.D. 534 are written in Greek. A good knowledge of Latin ceased to be a sine qua non for advancement in the imperial bureaucracy. We can be certain that Procopius learned his Latin at school, and later in life, when he went to Africa and Italy, he had plenty of opportunity to use it. But it is doubtful if he had any deep acquaintance with Latin literature or much interest in it. Latin was becoming a dead language in the East. Before it was refounded as the new Rome in 330, Constantinople had been the ancient Greek city of Byzantium, and it remained more Greek than Latin. When the University of Constantinople was begun in 425 under the emperor Theodosius II, fifteen professors were appointed to teach Greek language and literature compared with thirteen to teach Latin. But it was not until two and a half centuries later that the eastern empire abandoned Latin entirely.

Latin might be fading, but the heritage of classical Greece was a different matter. The classics were admired, studied in the schools, and imitated, not only for their own sake, but because they were still, in Procopius' youth, necessary for advancement in the imperial civil service. A law of Constantius II which is preserved in the Theodosian Code, stated: ". . . by no means shall any person obtain a place of the first order (in the guilds of imperial clerks) unless it is established that he excels in the practice and training of liberal studies, and that he is so polished in the use of letters that words proceed from him without the offense of imperfections, and it is Our will that all men be so informed. Moreover, in order that its rewards may not be denied to literature, which is the greatest of all virtues, if any man should appear to be worthy of the first place on account of his studies, and his skill in the use of words, Our provision shall make him of more honorable rank . . ."[11]

Cultivating "the greatest of all virtues" meant a sound knowledge of the classics. That they were a survival of the pagan world made no difference. In fact, the exercise books used by schoolboys in the fifth century are not substantially different from those used two centuries earlier. But the scholars were generally Christians, although pagan teachers were tolerated until Justinian banned them from all teaching posts, along with heretics and Samaritans, so that they might not (as Justinian's law put it) "drag contrarily the simpler persons' souls to their own error and in this way should make them lazier towards the orthodox persons' true and pure faith."[12] This law effectively meant the end of the University of Athens, the one school in the empire where pagan philosophy was still taught by pagans.

Justinian's objection was not to the pagan classics taught at Athens,[13] for they were taught everywhere, but to the religion of the teachers. For in the sixth century A.D., educated men still wrote in conscious imitation of their great predecessors a thousand years before them. They copied their style and their language; they even went so far as to write as if their readers were living in Periclean Athens. When they had to introduce words with which no classical Greek could have been familiar—for no contemporary of Pericles had heard of the various titles borne by imperial officials, much less of Christian bishops and the like—they did so with an explanation or a kind of apology.[14] The Byzantine empire maintained and defended its past, and its mission was restoration.

It was in this spirit that Justinian launched his program to renew the Roman *imperium*. The concept of *renovatio* was already old; Rome's greatest poet, Virgil, had written an eclogue five hundred years before Justinian's birth, in which he had invoked the idea in language which would remind Christians later of the prophet Isaiah. The same concept was to haunt the late Roman world, and occasionally it bursts forth in an imperial edict of Justinian. For instance, in 534, after Belisarius' fantastically successful campaign against the Vandals had restored Africa to the empire, he wrote:

The thanks and the praise we should offer to our Lord Jesus Christ my mind neither can conceive nor my tongue bring forth. Indeed before this we have had many gifts bestowed on us by God, and we confess to countless kindnesses given us, which we know we have done nothing to deserve. Yet greater than all is this, which omnipotent God has deemed worthy to make manifest through us for His praise and name: that Africa, made captive a hundred and five years ago by the Vandals has received its liberty in so short a time at our hands.[15]

And two years later, when Sicily had been recaptured and Byzantine armies were campaigning in Italy, Justinian expressed the hope that God would let him regain all the land which the ancient Romans had ruled from ocean to ocean, and which the negligence of their descendants had lost.[16]

II *The Age of Justinian*

Sometime about A.D. 470, three young Illyrian peasants from upper Macedonia left their home for Constantinople, traveling on foot, with some toasted bread rolled up in their cloaks for food. They left "after an unceasing struggle with poverty at home,"[17] writes Procopius, to whom we owe this information, and we may surmise the reason. The Huns had crossed the Vardar River in 447 and overrun the north of Greece as far as Thermopylae, and a few years later, the Ostrogoths had ravaged the same area, not leaving it in peace until 461. When these three young peasants reached the capital, they found that the emperor Leo was organizing a new body of palace guards, the *excubitores*, intended to counterbalance the excessive influence of the Germans in the army. Since they were young men of good physiques, they were promptly enrolled. Two of them disappeared from history at this point, but the third was to become the emperor Justin. We have few details of Justin's early career. Procopius tells a story of how one of his commanders, John the Hunchback, had imprisoned him for some misdemeanor and was about to execute him, when a vision appeared three times and warned John to release his prisoner.[18] We may be sure, however, that Justin was an able soldier, whose reputation increased until the emperor Anastasius appointed him commander of the *excubitores*. He held this strategic post in 518, when the emperor died without making arrangements for his successor. Justin remained illiterate as long as he lived, and after he became emperor himself, he had to use a stencil to affix the word *legi* to decrees in the imperial ink. (It was of a distinctive color.)[19] "His ignorance," remarks Gibbon, "was similar to that of Theodoric; and it is remarkable that, in an age not destitute of learning, two contemporary monarchs had never been instructed in the knowledge of the alphabet."[20] But illiteracy was the rule for the majority in the countryside and rural villages (we should not be led astray by the brilliance of a few centers of learning), and the fact that Justin came from a Latin-speaking area put him outside the main cultural stream of the Greek East. Yet he appreciated learning, and being childless himself, he saw to it that his family had the benefits of education. One member, Germanus, was to become a brilliant soldier. Another, the son of Justin's sister, Flavius Petrus Sabbatius, was adopted by Justin, and became the old man's Cardinal Richelieu. He is known to history by his adoptive name, Justinian.

Justin's accession on Anastasius' death was a stroke of good fortune. Anastasius had not intended his commander of the *excubitores* to succeed him, and he could scarcely have approved had he known, for he was a Monophysite and Justin was firmly orthodox. But the old emperor's most obvious heir, his nephew Hypatius, was absent, probably at Antioch[21]; Justin was in the capital, and his reputation for orthodoxy, the need for a quick decision, and a little judicious bribery, brought him the support of the Senate. The army and the people assembled in the Hippodrome and ratified the Senate's choice; and Justin was crowned.

He was already sixty-eight. Procopius' judgment of him was

that he managed to do his subjects neither harm nor good, for he was simply an easygoing country bumpkin. But the eminence behind the throne was Justinian, whose influence grew perhaps faster than the old man may have wished. When Procopius came to reckon up the years of Justinian's administration in his *Secret History,* he lumped Justin's reign in along with his successor's. Four months before his death, Justinian made his nephew co-emperor, and on August 1, 527, Justinian was left in sole control of the empire. He was then forty-five, and he was to rule for thirty-eight years.

If one of the duties of history is to distribute praise and blame, as many ancient historians believed, then the verdict on Justinian must be mixed. On the one hand, we have the Justinian who who codified the laws, restored Africa, Italy, and even a portion of Spain to the empire, trusting, as he said himself, "in the alliance of God," and who brought Byzantine architecture to its apogee. "The edifices of Justinian were cemented with the blood and treasure of his people," wrote Gibbon, with a characteristic turn of prose, but he was a little unfair. The church of the Holy Wisdom (Hagia Sophia) in Istanbul, now a museum, and the three churches in Ravenna with their famous mosaics, still remind us of the achievements of the age, and the *Codex Justinianus* remains a serious subject of study in continental Europe and Latin America, where Roman law is the basis of modern legal codes. If Justinian's attempt to renew the empire in the western Mediterranean proved terribly expensive and in the end, futile, it can be fairly said that this was for reasons which Justinian could hardly have foreseen when he started his campaigns.

On the other hand, we have the Justinian who threw himself with more energy than wisdom into theological disputes, which remained a passion throughout his life. Within two months of his uncle's accession, Justinian was writing to Pope Hormisdas summoning him to Constantinople to solve the Acacian schism. (We do not have the pope's reply, but he did not come.) Anastasius had favored the Monophysites as much as he dared, and his policies had resulted in a serious rebellion at the end of his reign. The policy of Justinian was generally orthodox. Only his wife Theodora continued to favor the Monophysites, and until her death from cancer in 548, she managed to mitigate her husband's intolerance and protect Monophysite churchmen; in fact, when she died, there was discovered in her quarters of the palace the patriarch Anthimius, who had been deposed twelve years earlier for heresy, and was presumed dead. Theodora had given him refuge virtually under her husband's nose!

Then there is Justinian the innovator, who marks the transition between the old Roman Empire and the Byzantine world. To quote from a recent book on Byzantium, more than any other ruler, he "was responsible for establishing the finished forms and setting the tone of Byzantine society which Diocletian had established."[22] From Augustus to Constantine the Great, the Roman Empire had been ruled by a partnership between the emperor and the Senate, however nominal it may have been at times. Constantine substituted the Christian church as his partner. Justinian practically dispensed with the partner. Agathias of Myrrhina, who continued Procopius' *History of the Wars,* labeled Justinian "the first autocrat in deed as well as name."[23] Officially, he was styled *autocrator,* the Greek translation of the Latin *imperator,* but his usual title, by which he appears in Procopius, was *basileus,* or "king," the title borne by Alexander the Great and his successors. (The old Latin term for "king," *rex,* was, Procopius tells us, what the barbarians called their leaders.) A century later, *basileus* was to become the official title of the emperor,[24] but his power was autocratic.

Finally, there is Justinian the oppressor, a man of "insatiable avarice," as he was characterized by a historian who was a boy during his reign.[25] Procopius claims that Anastasius left a surplus of 3,200 *centenaria* of gold in the treasury at his death, but it did not last long. Justinian's policies were expensive. However, some of the greatest disasters of Justinian's reign were what modern insurance underwriters would define as acts of God. Between 526 and 557, nine earthquakes are recorded; the last of these, on December 14, 557, shook the fabric of the new church of Hagia Sophia so severely that it partially collapsed a few months later.[26] Worse than the earthquakes was the bubonic plague, which appeared in epidemic form for the first time that we can record it with certainty in Europe. In 542, Constantinople was stricken, and Procopius, who was there at the time, has left a graphic description modeled on Thucydides' account of the plague which struck

Athens in 430 B.C. But whatever Thucydides' plague may have been, typhus fever, measles, smallpox, or some other candidate, it was probably not bubonic plague, whose distinguishing symptom is swellings in the groin and armpits, caused by enlarged lymph glands. The plague recurred sporadically through the sixth century, then disappeared to recur only in the fourteenth century as the Black Death.

Epidemics, like wars, are usually accompanied by an increased number of marriages and a spurt in the birth rate. Hence, whatever population losses the epidemic causes are soon made up. However, bubonic plague is particularly fatal to pregnant women, and wherever it has struck in historical times, the increased marriage rate has always been followed by a high death rate among young brides, with the result that the population has not been easily restored after the plague subsided. In the eastern Mediterranean, the population had been reasonably stable since the first century A.D.; the only area where it declined substantially was Egypt. The plague of the mid-sixth century cut it sharply by 20 to 25 percent in the first few years, which was followed by a slower decline to about 60 percent of the pre-plague total by the year 600.[27] These figures are estimates, of course, calculated in part by analogy with the Black Death, but we have no reason to doubt their approximate validity.

Even without this calamity, Justinian's policies would have strained the resources of the empire. As it was, the plague meant fewer recruits for the army and fewer taxpayers to bear the increasing demands of the treasury for revenue. Procopius complains bitterly that, far from lightening taxation when the plague was sweeping the empire, Justinian made surviving landowners responsible for the taxes of their deceased neighbors.[28] As for the army, the evidence suggests that it had to rely more and more on barbarian troops,[29] although they were better integrated than was the case in the late fourth century, when Rome had had to turn to barbarian federate troops for her own protection. Even so, imperial forces fell woefully below strength. Agathias describes the situation in 558: "Although there ought to have been a total strength to muster of 645,000 fighting men, at that time, the number stood barely at 150,000."[30] All of this makes more remarkable Justinian's military achievements, as Procopius de-

scribes them, but it also puts into perspective his growing disillusion which we may detect in the *History of the Wars of Justinian.*
Charles Diehl, in his *Justinien et la Civilization Byzantine au
VIe Siècle,* published at the beginning of this century, called our
attention to a distinction which he was not the first to make,
between the younger and the older Justinian, the Justinian before
the plague of 542 (he was gravely ill himself) and Justininan
afterward, or else the Justinian before Theodora died in 548, and
the aging emperor who carried on after her death, becoming
more and more deeply embroiled in theological issues. Diehl
pointed to two contemporary mosaics depicting Justinian; and
although one of these is no longer accepted as a reliable likeness,
it may still be of some value to repeat the comparison.[31] The
earlier is in the church of San Vitale in Ravenna, and dates to
547, when Justinian was sixty-five. However, official portraits
rarely keep up with the developing wrinkles and gray hairs of
their subjects, and the Justinian of San Vitale is a man in his
prime, vigorous and alert, with a direct, compelling gaze. The
second portrait, also in Ravenna, is in San Apollinare Nuovo, a
church which was originally built under the Ostrogoths and then
transferred from the Arian to Catholic rite after the Byzantine
conquest. The portrait, if it were reliable, would show Justinian
about ten years later, with a double chin, and a dreamy, even
hypocritical gaze. However, it is generally believed now that this
mosaic was originally a likeness of Theodoric, which was reused
as a portrait of Justinian when the church was rededicated, and
the historian must approach it with caution. Yet it bears a certain
resemblance to Procopius' description of the emperor: "neither
tall in stature nor very short, but of medium height, yet not thin,
but somewhat plump. . . . To describe his general appearance,
he bore a very close resemblance to Domitian, the son of Vespasian . . ."[32] A bust of Domitian placed beside the San
Apollinare portrait shows a resemblance worth remarking.

We may accept Diehl's conclusion without the portrait he
used to illustrate it. The aging emperor was no longer the vigorous
man who had launched a program to renew the empire, whose
defenses decayed while he turned his energies more and more to
defining the nature of God. He found the answer at last in an
extreme form of heresy called Monothelitism, which he tried to

establish as orthodox doctrine, and only his death averted a conflict with the church.

But whether or not Justinian himself was great, his reign was a period of greatness. He appointed and encouraged brilliant generals to lead his armies, such as Belisarius, who conquered the Vandals with a handful of men; Narses, the eunuch who finally defeated the Ostrogoths; and his own cousin, Germanus. Under Justinian's direction, great jurists such as Tribonian from the University of Constantinople and Dorotheus from the law school at Berytus codified the laws. The church of Hagia Sophia still stands as a monument to the genius of the engineers Anthemius of Tralles and Isidore of Miletus, who built it. Procopius himself was the greatest historian that the Byzantine Empire produced: a writer who invites comparison with Herodotus and Thucydides. His *History* was continued on to 558 by Agathias, a lesser figure, who was a poet as well as a historian, and who has left behind an anthology of epigrams. Menander Protector, who continued Agathias, survives only in fragments. The collection of Greek epigrams known as the Palatine anthology (the manuscript was housed in the Palatine library in Heidelberg) contains some 376 poems from this period, by men such as Agathias, Paul the Silentiary, and lesser figures described as lawyers, public officials, and even a *grammaticus.* The same manuscript preserves a long poem by Paul the Silentiary on the restoration of Hagia Sophia in 562, after its partial collapse four years before. It is in hexameters, the meter of Homer and Virgil. The example of the past lay heavily on these men; yet at the same time, the greatest of Byzantine hymn writers, Romanus Melodus, was composing religious poetry in the Greek spoken on the streets, not in the vocabulary of the classical past.

Procopius stands above them all. All his works have survived: his *History of the Wars of Justinian,* the *Buildings* and the *Secret History.* The *Secret History* has raised doubts. As soon as it was exhumed from the Vatican Library and published in 1623, it became the center of a dispute with Catholic theologians and historians ranged on one side, and Protestant theologians and jurists on the other. The former were happy to accept the authenticity of the *Secret History,* for they regarded Justinian and, even more, Theodora, as archenemies of the papacy, and were delighted to find their wickedness so explicitly set forth. In fact, its first editor, Alemannus, remarked that it was not worthwhile to seek evidence to confirm the *Secret History,* for nothing was too execrable to be believed of a woman who tried to overturn the Council of Chalcedon. But wherever Roman law was studied, Justinian was respected, and the jurists, who saw Justinian as the champion of the rights of the state, were determined to defend his memory. They rejected the *Secret History* as a forgery.

However, the style and language of this libelous little pamphlet have been examined carefully, and as a result, scholars now generally accept it as a genuine work of Procopius.[33] Curious and amazing though it is, it is still a product of the psychology of the age; and because we possess it, we are forced to remember the seamy side of the glories of Justinian.

III   *The Life of Procopius*

Neither the exact date of Procopius' birth nor of his death is known with any certainty.[34] However, his home was Caesarea in Palestine—"my Caesarea," as he calls it in a passage in the *Secret History*—and we can assume that he was born there between 490 and 500. He tells us nothing about his family. About the time he was born, the governor of Palestine, with his seat at Caesarea, was one Procopius of Edessa, and the historian, who mentions him once, calls him a "learned man."[35] It is tempting to believe that he was a relative, but it is pressing coincidence too far to think that they were father and son. All we can say is that Procopius speaks from the viewpoint of the landowning class in his *Secret History,* and we can guess with fair certainty that this was the class into which he was born.

The population of Caesarea was largely Greek, or at least people who had been assimilated into the Greek cultural stream. The Jewish population had been exterminated in the Jewish revolt of A.D. 66, and although we may believe that some Jews had returned, their numbers cannot have been great. However, there was a large population of Samaritans, who were to rise in rebellion in 529 and again in 555. Yet even these, if they lived in the city, seem to have been partially assimilated and not to have taken their religion too seriously. When Justinian attempted to enforce religious orthodoxy throughout the empire, "the Samaritans who lived in my own Caesarea," wrote Procopius, "and the other cities [in Palestine] thought it silly to suffer any discomfort for a foolish belief, and they adopted the name of Christians in place of what they then bore, and by this subterfuge succeeded in freeing themselves from the danger of the law."[36] However, the Samaritans who lived in the rural areas adopted a more rigorous attitude.

Procopius' native language was Greek, the lingua franca of the Hellenized East since the third century B.C. In his youth, Latin was still necessary for the study of law, although even at the famous law school at Berytus, some lectures were being given in Greek. By the middle of the century, Greek was replacing Latin as the working language of the imperial bureaucracy. There can be no doubt about Procopius' proficiency in Latin, although there is no indication that he took any interest in Latin literature. Few Greeks did; they had enough literature of their own. We have less evidence for Procopius' knowledge of other languages. He may have known Syriac, for he quotes from a history of Armenia written in Syriac by Faustus of Buzanta,[37] and unless he learned the contents of this work at second-hand, he must have known Syriac himself. Persian is unlikely, although Procopius can interpret a few Persian terms. The army to which he was attached for at least twelve years and perhaps longer, was a medley of racial groups and tongues, and he could have picked up a smattering of a number of languages.[38]

As a center of learning, Caesarea yielded to her neighbors, Alexandria in Egypt, and Gaza, but still it was the civil capital of Palestine, the seat of the metropolitan bishop, and the possessor of a famous library founded by the great Origen. However, we are probably right in thinking that Procopius attended school at Gaza, which was connected with Caesarea by an ancient road along the coast. Gaza was at the height of its brilliance, a little island of classical learning which stood aloof from the theological disputes absorbing the energies of scholars in neighboring Alexandria and Antioch. In fact, under Justinian, Gaza was the only center of literary production outside Constantinople. Although the names of writers such as Procopius (called "of Gaza" to distinguish him from the historian), Choricius, Aeneas, and Marcianus, are virtually unknown now, they were famous men of letters in their day. The curriculum of the Gaza school laid heavy emphasis on the Greek classics, on Herodotus, Thucydides, and the orators in particular. Students were well grounded in the rules of rhetoric and could turn out neat panegyrics in the approved manner if the need arose. There were also Christian writings on the syllabus, for Gaza had adjusted to the Christian world, and among the writings of Procopius of Gaza we find various religious works, including a commentary on Isaiah; and his fellow schoolman, Aeneas of Gaza, wrote a dialogue in which he imagined Aristotle's disciple, Theophrastus, becoming convinced by Christian arguments about immortality and resurrection.[39]

The historian Procopius was a product of this kind of education, and although we are told nowhere explicitly that he attended school at Gaza, we are probably safe to assume that he did. However, he passed on after graduation to study law, which meant a four, or more probably a five-year course at a recognized law school, and at Berytus, not far from Caesarea was one of the most famous of these, where possibly Procopius was a student.[40] In any case, he became a *rhetor,* that is, a professional pleader or attorney at law, and later, when he came to write his *Secret History,* one of his bitterest criticisms attacked Justinian's judicial reforms whereby he reduced the perquisites of the *rhetores.* A *rhetor* who built up a reputation could make a very comfortable living. Procopius mentions one of them, belonging, as it happened, to Caesarea, who became so wealthy that he was able to buy a village by the seashore as an investment, and by so doing attracted the cupidity of the emperor.[41]

Procopius appears in history in 527, the year that Justinian ascended the throne. From then until 542, we can document his activities with few gaps. Shortly before Justin's death, an army under Libellarius, commander of the imperial fortress of Daras on the eastern frontier, had invaded Persian territory near Nisibis, and then retreated precipitously, although it met no resistance. Thereupon the emperor replaced Libellarius with Belisarius, a promising young officer picked out of his own bodyguards. "At that time," noted Procopius, by way of introducing himself, "there was chosen as his advisor, Procopius, who wrote this history."[42]

His position was legal secretary or *assessor,*[43] and how he came to be chosen for this post we do not know; in some way he must have come to the emperor's notice. However, his duties were to keep him at Belisarius' side through his campaigns in the East, and then to take him to Africa and Italy until 540. After that, we are not certain what his contacts were with his old general, but it is clear that his feelings toward Belisarius were changing from admiration to disgust and bitterness.

In 530, Belisarius, now in command of the whole eastern front, moved against the Persians and defeated them at Daras. Procopius' description of this battle in his *History of the Wars* is an eyewitness account which may have been based on his own official report. Next year, Belisarius was less fortunate; he was defeated at Callinicum and recalled to the capital. Procopius passes over a piece of information which we learn from another source: that Justinian sent out an official to investigate the defeat, and states rather that the emperor intended Belisarius to lead an expedition against the Vandal kingdom in Africa. We need not assume that the investigation placed any blame on Belisarius, for he seems to have lost none of Justinian's confidence. However, the recall meant that Belisarius and, along with him, Procopius, were in Constantinople in January of 532, when the Nika riots broke out there, and nearly toppled Justinian's regime.

Procopius' account is again that of an eyewitness. He does not tell us explicitly that he was besieged in the palace along with the imperial court, but he does give verbatim the little speech which the empress Theodora made when her husband and his advisors had decided to give up, embark on ship, and flee for their lives: "If you want to save yourself, O emperor, there is nothing to prevent you. We have plenty of money. There is the sea, and here are the ships. As for me, I like the old proverb, that the imperial purple makes a fine winding-sheet." It is a splendid scene and a courageous speech, although perhaps we should remember that for a man with a good classical education, Theodora's little proverb about the imperial purple making a good winding sheet recalled a similar scene almost a thousand years earlier when a tyrant with an evil reputation was besieged by his rebellious subjects and called together his advisors to decide what to do. One told him that tyranny was a fair winding sheet.[44] In any case, Justinian regained his nerve and ordered Belisarius and Mundus, another able young officer who was in the capital, to attack the rioters, and the uprising ended in a bloody massacre in the Hippodrome.

The expedition to Africa got under way in 533, with Belisarius in command, accompanied by his wife, Antonina.

And with them was also Procopius, who wrote this history. Earlier he had been frightened at the danger, but later he saw a vision in a dream which encouraged him, and made him eager for the expedition. For in his dream, he imagined he was in Belisarius' house, and one of his servants came in and announced that some men had come with gifts. And Belisarius ordered him to see what sort of gifts they were, and he went into the court and saw men who were carrying earth with flowers on their shoulders. He ordered these men to bring into the house the earth which they had brought, and set it in the portico; and Belisarius came there with his guardsmen, and reclined on the earth himself and urged others to do the same. As they reclined and ate as if on a couch, the food seemed to them very sweet.[45]

Procopius does not elaborate further. He belonged to an age which understood visions, and the fruitful earth which was presented to Belisarius in the dream was the earth of Africa.

Procopius speaks of himself again in his *History* when the fleet reached Sicily. Wanting to discover the best place to land on the African coast, and to see if the Vandals were preparing to meet him, Belisarius sent Procopius to Syracuse ostensibly to buy supplies but in fact to glean information. There Procopius happened to meet a childhood friend from Caesarea, now a merchant in Syracuse whose ships shuttled back and forth to Africa. One of his men had returned from Carthage only three days before and reported that the Vandals suspected nothing. "For," writes Procopius, "no one had given them information that an army was coming against them at this time. . . . Hence Gelimer without thought of war, and paying no attention to Carthage and all other places on the sea, was staying at Hermione, which is in Byzacium, four days' journey from the coast."

Thereupon Procopius contrived to kidnap his friend's informant, and took him to the fleet, where Belisarius was delighted with the news he brought. The signal for departure was given; the fleet sailed for Libya and landed at Caputvada (Shoal's Head), a "five days' journey from Carthage for an unencumbered man."[46]

All went well. Belisarius defeated the Vandal king Gelimer in mid-September in a battle fought ten miles outside Carthage, entered the city, and in Gelimer's palace, dined with his officers on food which had been prepared for the enemy the day before. "One could see Fortune in her glory," remarked Procopius, who witnessed the scene, "and making a show of the fact that everything is in her power, and nothing is the private possession of man."[47] Gelimer surrendered the following spring, and the Vandal kingdom came to an end. Handing over the command in Africa to Solomon, Belisarius returned to Constantinople with his captives and the Vandal treasure, including loot which the founder of the Vandal kingdom, Gaiseric, had taken when he pillaged Rome almost a century before.

Procopius remained behind. At least he was in Africa in early 536, when the Byzantine army there mutinied, and he escaped along with Solomon and a handful of men to Sicily. There he rejoined Belisarius. The campaign against the Ostrogothic kingdom in Italy had already started, and as the first act, Belisarius had been sent to reconquer Sicily. But when Solomon and Procopius arrived to ask for his help, he selected one hundred men, and taking Solomon with him, he sailed for Carthage with one ship to set affairs in order.

Procopius does not say that he went along. Probably he stayed behind in Sicily. In any case, Belisarius was soon recalled by the news that his own army had mutinied. The rebellion in Africa was not settled until Justinian finally sent his own cousin Germanus to deal with the situation. For the next four years, Procopius was to remain on Belisarius' staff during the campaign in Italy which ended with the fall of Ravenna in 540.

Occasionally, Procopius inserts some autobiographical information into his books on the Gothic wars. At one point, he tells how he examined the Sibylline oracles in Rome: proof, if we needed it, that he had a good working knowledge of Latin. Perhaps he was acting in his official capacity as Belisarius' *assessor* when he examined these oracles. In any case, his verdict was that they were worthless guides for the future.[48] Again, when Belisarius was besieged in Rome by the Gothic king Wittigis he dispatched Procopius to Naples to collect men and supplies, and a little later, when he learned that Procopius had managed to get out of the beleaguered city and circumvent the Gothic army, he sent his wife to join him. Procopius carried out his mission at Naples and joined a small relief army which had just arrived. About the time of the winter solstice, this relief force reached Rome.[49]

As the campaign dragged on, Procopius noted the suffering of the Italians. The land could not be cultivated because of the marching and countermarching of armies, and in the district of Picenum, Procopius estimated that fifty thousand farmers died of famine. Some turned to cannibalism. Procopius retails a story of how two women, living north of Ariminum, ate seventeen men. Strangers passing through their village would lodge at their house, for they were the only survivors living in the place, and while their lodgers slept, the two women killed and ate them. The eighteenth lodger awoke in time to see what was happening, leaped out of his bed and after extracting their story from them, slew the murderous ladies.[50] There is a certain bitter piquancy to a story which Procopius reports early in his *Gothic Wars* with the Herodotean caveat that he cannot vouch for its accuracy. Theodatus, a weak, vicious man who was king of the Ostrogoths when the Byzantine forces initiated the campaign (the Goths soon exchanged him for Wittigis, who was abler, but no match for Belisarius) asked a Jew with a reputation for prophecy what the outcome of the war would be. The Jew told him to take thirty swine, divide them into groups of ten, and call these groups the Goths, the Romans (that is, the natives of Italy), and the soldiers of the emperor. Then he should shut up these three herds of swine in three separate huts without food and wait a few days. Theodatus did as he was instructed, and at the appointed time he and the Jew went to the huts and found that, of the Goths, all but two were dead. Most of the emperor's soldiers were still alive. As for the Romans, all their hair had fallen out, but half were still living.[51]

Belisarius captured Ravenna in 540, and the victory seemed complete. "And while I was watching the Roman army enter Ravenna then," Procopius wrote, "the thought crossed my mind that it is not by the cleverness of men or some other virtue of theirs that events are brought to pass, but that there is some divine power which is always warping their purposes, and twisting them so that there will be no hindrance to our destined ends."[52] Belisarius returned to Constantinople with the Gothic king Wittigis captive, and the leadership of the Byzantine forces fell into lesser hands. Very soon, the Goths had a new king, Totila, whom Procopius invested with all the qualities of moderation and leadership which he once saw in Belisarius, and the war in Italy flared up again.

From this point on, we can no longer trace Procopius' movements with any certainty. No doubt he returned to Constantinople with Belisarius; but when his old commander campaigned on the Persian front in 541, we do not know if Procopius was still on his staff. However, we know that he was in Constantinople in 542, for that was the year of the plague, which Procopius claims to have witnessed.[53] A story in the *Secret History* leads us to suspect that this may also have been the time when Procopius' final break with Belisarius came. Justinian fell ill with the plague, and during his illness a number of his officers began to talk about the succession in a way that was complimentary neither to the emperor nor the empress. After Justinian recovered, there was an investigation. Although nothing was proved against Belisarius, he was relieved of his command, and many of his old friends were forbidden to visit him.[54] Procopius does not indicate how this prohibition affected him personally, but from 542 on, he seems to have been not quite so fully informed about the events of Justinian's wars as hitherto. He had been an insider as *assessor* of Belisarius; now he was relegated to the sidelines.

He was still fairly knowledgeable about what was going on in Italy, and he was highly critical of the Byzantine officers there. Yet we have only one shred of evidence to suggest that he ever revisited Italy himself: when he comes to describe the twelfth year of the Gothic War (546-547), his narrative suddenly becomes noticeably more detailed. This has led one scholar to suggest that he made a brief visit to Italy in 546.[55] We do not know. Yet, he was by now an inveterate traveler, and there is real regret implicit in one of the digressions which, in Herodotean fashion, he inserted on the island of Thule (Iceland, or perhaps the northern Scandinavian peninsula): "And although I was eager to go to this island and become an eyewitness of the things I have been told, I had no opportunity."[56] However, it was during this period that he was writing his *History of the Wars of Justinian* in seven books, dealing with events up to 550. The finished work was published in its entirety in 551.

Yet before the *History* reached its final form, Procopius probably gave public readings of parts of it and possibly even produced written versions of certain sections. One part which stands out like a prose *chanson de geste* is the description of the great siege of Rome, when the Gothic king Wittigis shut Belisarius in the city over the winter of 537-38. It contains a clue which tells us when it was written. Procopius described how a Byzantine officer was shot in the face with an arrow, so that the iron point penetrated his head and disappeared entirely. The man lived on, feeling no discomfort. But in the fifth year after he was shot, the tip of the arrow began to project visibly from his face. And, writes Procopius, "this is now the third year that it has been slowly but steadily coming out."[57] If we count the years on our fingers, "the third year" cannot be later than 544. This was the year that Belisarius, restored to imperial favor, was sent back to Italy to carry on the war against the Goths. The account of his heroic defense of Rome must have made a flattering bon voyage. Perhaps it was even a hint that Procopius was ready for an invitation to return to his old post.

A few years after Procopius published the seven books of the *History of the Wars,* he undertook to continue his narrative and produced an eighth book, which brought the history to the end of 552 and to the ultimate defeat of the Goths at the hands of Narses, a eunuch for whom Procopius had no great liking, though he grants that Narses was able and popular with his men. The tone of this last book is more openly critical; at one point Procopius states openly that Justinian had conducted the war in Italy negligently. Stranger, perhaps, is the favorable picture he gives of the Gothic king Totila, and the heroism with which he invests the Goths as they go down to final destruction before the Byzantine forces.

Procopius produced two other works, but when they were written is a separate question which we will examine in the next section. Suffice it to say that even if we had only the *History of the Wars of Justinian,* we would have reason to believe that, as Procopius grew older, he became increasingly disillusioned and critical of Justinian's policies. The Procopius who joined Belisarius' staff at Daras in 527 seems to have been filled with admiration for his commander and to have been reasonably optimistic about the emperor's program. As time went on, the optimism faded, and admiration eventually gave way to bitterness. Perhaps the cost of Justinian's wars in money and human suffering made its impression, or perhaps personal disappointment played a part. Yet it seems that he continued to enjoy some imperial favor. In the introduction to the *Buildings,* which was commissioned by the emperor, there is the intriguing statement that men "who have been well-treated at the hands of their rulers have been grateful to their benefactors and have returned thank-offerings to them."[58] Had Procopius himself received some benefaction from Justinian? At some point in his career, we know that Justinian had conferred on him the rank of *illustris,* which put him in the inner circle of the aristocracy. Yet the *Buildings* is a cold eulogy, and we can catch the occasional ambiguity behind its formal praises which perhaps indicates what Procopius' true feelings were about Justinian.

We do not know when he died. The *Buildings* is unfinished; he may have died while he was working at it. He mentions at one point that he intended to write something on theological disputes, but as as far as we know, he never did.[59] A Procopius was prefect of Constantinople in 562, but the name was not uncommon, and we need not believe that this was Procopius the historian. I am inclined to think that he died not much later than 560, for reasons which I will set out in the next section.

As a writer, Procopius belongs to the great Byzantine school of "secular historians," a group labeled much more expressively by German scholars as *profanhistoriker,* but the obvious English translation, "profane historians," conveys an inaccurate impression. So the label "secular historians," will have to do. As a literary genre, secular history was a by-product of the Christianization of the empire. That is to say, both secular and Christian history developed out of the ideological battles of the fourth century, after Constantine the Great had given the Christian church semiofficial status but before the cause of paganism seemed irretrievably lost.

The first practitioners of secular history were pagans: men like Eunapius, Ammianus Marcellinus, and Zosimus. Ammianus, a Greek who wrote in Latin, was cool but neutral; Zosimus made no secret of his view that Christianity was ruining the empire; and Eunapius' history of the fourth century was so hostile to the Christians that it had to be re-edited. The weapons of the secular historians were prose style and the traditions of classical historiography, which had been founded by Herodotus and Thucydides. To the modern reader, the secular historians often seem more attractive than their counterparts of the opposite school. Jacob Burckhardt said of Eusebius of Caesarea, the first man to write specifically Christian history, and the founder of the type, that he was "the first thoroughly dishonest historian of antiquity." Yet the pagans fought a losing battle, and as we have seen, the final mopping-up took place under Justinian.[60]

Yet secular history as a genre survived, continued by Christian writers. The statement still appears now and then in general studies of the eastern empire that Procopius was half pagan because the attitude he adopts seems to belong to the pre-Christian world; but this view does not stand up to examination. Christianity had not accommodated itself to classical culture without a struggle, but by the sixth century, the accommodation was made. Although the authors who continued to produce secular history dropped the anti-Christian tone, they saw no need to change the other traditions of the school.

They looked to the past for their models, not so much the immediate past as to the great age of classical Greece. Procopius' language was intended to be acceptable in the literary circles of Periclean Athens, in spite of the thousand years which separated it from Justinian's Constantinople, where the language spoken on the streets had already evolved part way toward modern Greek. But Procopius would never have considered taking his language from the streets. On the contrary, we find phrases borrowed bodily from Herodotus and Thucydides. Where Procopius must introduce words not found in his models, he inserts a "so-called" or an "as they call it," to indicate that he uses the word under constraint, for lack of anything more classical. We have "so-called *referendarii*," a "so-called *quaesitor*," and, surprisingly, even an explanation of what a Roman legion was.[61] Christian terminology needed interpretation too, for neither Herodotus nor Thucydides knew anything about Christianity, and they had no vocabulary to deal with it. We find Procopius explaining that *ekklesia,* the word for a Christian church, is the equivalent of a temple or shrine, and monks are "the most temperate of Christians . . . whom men are accustomed to call 'monks.' "[62] The great church of Hagia Sophia is called at one point "the sanctuary of Christ the great God . . . 'Sophia' [wisdom] the Byzantines call the temple, believing this designation especially appropriate to God."[63] The detachment with which Procopius writes is surprising. Yet we should accept it for what it is: a literary mask, a style which was the mark of a well-educated, cultured man. We should not believe that he was a fractional pagan because we sometimes find him writing about Christian churchmen with the same detachment that Herodotus wrote about the Egyptians or the Scythians. There may be other grounds for thinking that Procopius' attitude toward the theological disputes of his day was that of a somewhat skeptical pragmatist, but we cannot base this conclusion on his literary style.

This classical mask which Procopius assumed had one great advantage, and, from our point of view at least, one disadvantage. The advantage was that, from behind his mask, he could write with greater freedom; under the pretense that he was following his classical models, he could even upon occasion criticize imperial policy. In the Byzantine empire, criticism was rarely welcome, but it was more likely to be acceptable if written with literary taste. This disadvantage is that the effort to see events through the eyes of classical models may have resulted in some distortion. When we find an incident described in Procopius in a way that closely parallels something similar in Thucydides, can we be certain that Procopius has not altered the truth a little to make the parallel more striking? This is a question we must take up later. For the moment, it is well to recall that one of the traditions of secular history held that it was the proper function of a historian to describe events as they really happened, that is, to tell the truth. We find Procopius repeating this time-worn principle in the introduction to his *History of the Wars*: "For he [Procopius] believed that cleverness is appropriate to rhetoric and relating fanciful stories to poetry, but truth is what is fitting for history."[64] Of course, even for the best historians, truth is not invariably absolute.

IV *The Dates of Procopius' Works*

A discussion of dates is rarely stimulating; nevertheless the question of when Procopius composed and published his various works is too important to avoid. It is also one which has attracted a good deal of scholarly dispute.[65] The *History of the Wars of Justinian* presents the fewest difficulties. The first seven books were published together, as Procopius tells us himself, and this means that they could not have appeared before 551, for Procopius does not break off his account of the Gothic War before the end of 550. However, they cannot have appeared much later, for there is no hint that Procopius was aware as yet that the Gothic campaign would end with a decisive victory in 552. Probably what happened is this: the first two books dealing with the Persian War up to 549 (there is, however, a reference which must indicate that Procopius was adding a finishing touch to the first book in 550) appeared earliest, in late 550 or in the new year, followed in rapid succession by the two books on the Vandalic War and the three books on the Gothic War.

Yet when Procopius wrote the *History of the Wars,* he did not start at the beginning and go to the end. The plan he adopted did not allow for any such procedure, for he chose to deal with the three wars in which he took part in separate geographical divisions, the first dealing with the East, the second with Africa, and the third with Italy.[66] But it is hard to believe that Procopius had any such plan in mind when he first conceived his idea of writing a history, which may have been about 533, when the Vandal expedition was under way; for only after this point do we get personal reminiscences, indicating that he was keeping notes for future use. Rather, he probably started by writing an account of those military operations in which he participated himself; in support of this view, it is worth noting that he claims proudly in his introduction that he had the good fortune to "be an eyewitness at nearly all the events which took place." Now Procopius was on the eastern front from 527 to 531, in Africa from 533 to 536, and in Italy until 540. If his initial plan was to write a history based on his own experiences, what he would have produced would have been an account of operations on the Persian frontier until 531 (in 532, Persia and Byzantium signed a so-called Endless Peace), followed by events in Africa up to 536, and by the Gothic campaign up to the surrender of Ravenna. Procopius could have claimed honestly that he had been an eyewitness to all these events and need not have qualified his statement. It would have made a very nice history, which might have been subtitled "The Triumphs of Belisarius."

Although my view is based on conjecture, I suspect that this was the history which Procopius at first intended to write. However, he changed his mind. There may have been more than one reason why he did so. One reason was certainly artistic; a general history of the wars on all fronts was more ambitious than a personal memoir, more worthy of comparison with Herodotus and Thucydides. Another reason may have been apprehension. Procopius may have realized that Justinian would not welcome a history which attributed his victories so generously to Belisarius (Justinian himself attributed them to God),[67] and perhaps more important was the fact that Belisarius' triumphs appeared increasingly ephemeral as time went on. The Goths, defeated in 540, rallied under Totila and the struggle in Italy continued. The Persians broke the "Endless Peace" and wreaked havoc on Syria, while in Africa, the Byzantine forces, having vanquished the Vandals, had to deal with the Moors who proved more difficult. Procopius' history had a beginning but no ending.

Thus, when Procopius began to put together the *History* for publication after his return to Constantinople, he took the notes he had already written and re-edited them to fit into a plan which fell into the three sections we now have. Yet the editing was not so thorough that we cannot see the author's blue pencil at work. The history of the war in Africa ends for practical purposes in 545, and probably this section was finished then. However, five years later, Procopius added a few more lines which brought the narrative down to 549. Both books of the *Persian War* deal in their concluding paragraphs with the fall of Justinian's praetorian prefect, John the Cappadocian, and both of these sections look as if they were added just before publication. On the other hand, the parts dealing with the war against the Persians prior to the "Endless Peace," as well as Belisarius' campaign against the Vandals, must belong to the early portions of the *History*.

The introduction with which Procopius begins the eighth book of the *Wars of Justinian* makes it clear that the first seven books had already been published when it appeared. One passage allows us to date it with some precision. In 545, Justinian made a five-year treaty with the Persians, according to which he was to pay them twenty *centenaria* (2,000 pounds) of gold. In 550, the treaty expired, and it was renewed eighteen months later for another twenty *centenaria* (four per year, but Justinian paid the Persians in a lump sum to avoid the appearance of paying tribute), plus six *centenaria* for the eighteen months between the second treaty and the expiry of the first. In his description of these negotiations, Procopius breaks out indignantly that up to his time, over a space of eleven years, six months, the Persians had collected forty-six *centenaria* of gold.[68] This period of eleven years, six months, must start with 545, and hence it was not before 556 that Procopius wrote the passage in question. The eighth book probably appeared, then, in 557.

The dates of the last two works, the *Buildings* and the *Secret History*, present their own problems. Until recently, the accepted date for the *Buildings* was 560, and it was based on a passage where Procopius describes the construction of a bridge in Asia Minor,[69] which was proceeding apace. From another source, later but reasonably reliable, we learn that this bridge was started in 559–60 A.D.[70] Hence the date 560.

But if this date for the *Buildings* is right, then Procopius makes some interesting omissions. In the first book, he describes the construction of the church of Hagia Sophia in Constantinople, and he extols it as evidence of the divine inspiration which animated the emperor. When engineering problems involved in erecting the great dome baffled the master builders, they turned to Justinian for guidance, and he told them what they should do.[71] But Procopius neglects to mention that this dome collapsed on May 7, 558, and by 560, rebuilding was under way. Then too, Procopius pretends that most of the Samaritans in his native Palestine were contented converts to Christianity,[72] whereas their discontent was such that they revolted in 555. And it has also been pointed out that Procopius extols Justinian for spreading peace and Christianity among wild frontier tribesmen called the Tzani,[73] whereas in fact we know that after 557 the Tzani returned to brigandage. So the argument goes that the *Buildings* must date before 555, the evidence of the bridge notwithstanding.[74]

But we must remember that the *Buildings* was intended as a panegyric, and panegyrics are not marked by devotion to the whole truth. If Procopius omitted mention of the Samaritan revolt, or the lawlessness of the ungrateful Tzani, he may only have been following the niceties of his literary genre. But his failure to say anything about the collapse of Hagia Sophia is more surprising. He describes the erection of the great dome which crowned the church in terms that implied it was proof of the emperor's divine inspiration, and this would scarcely have seemed the proper approach to take after the dome had fallen. We do not expect accuracy in panegyrics, but neither do we expect irony. Moreover, unlike the Tzani and the Samaritans who were far away, Hagia Sophia was hard to ignore. Its ruins were virtually outside the palace windows.

Perhaps the right solution is to believe that Procopius wrote the first book of the *Buildings* containing his description of Hagia Sophia before the dome collapsed on May 7, 558. The books which followed may be slightly later, but the first book remained unrevised. In any case, we have good reason to think that the *Buildings* was never finished, for although Procopius declares his intention to describe Justinian's building program throughout his whole empire, he concludes abruptly without mentioning Italy at all. It is hard to account for the omission in any other way than by believing that Procopius failed to complete his treatise.

But if the *Buildings* is unfinished, what is the reason? It is possible that the emperor, who commissioned the work,[75] lost interest, and Procopius abandoned it. But it is considerably more probable that Procopius died before he could complete it. If so, we have a probable date for his death: not long after 560.

The *Secret History* had no publication date during Justinian's lifetime, for obvious reasons. In fact, it is mentioned nowhere until the tenth century, when the *Souda* lists it among Procopius' works under the title *Anekdota* (Unpublished Works) and treats it as the final book of the *History of the Wars*. And so in a sense it is. If we compare the opening paragraph of the *Secret History* with that of the eighth book of the *Wars,* the similarity of the wording is striking. The one virtually quotes the other. However, this does not prove that the *Secret History* was written later than book eight of the *Wars.* Even though the *Secret History* was unpublished, Procopius himself could have quoted from it any time he pleased, so long as he did not give himself away.

Within the *Secret History* itself, there is what appears to be good evidence for its date of composition. On four occasions,[76] Procopius speaks of Justinian's having administered the empire for thirty-two years. If this is thirty-two years from 527, when Justinian became emperor, then the *Secret History* was composed between mid-558 and 559,[77] when, as we have seen, Procopius was probably at work on his *Buildings.* But it is clear that the secret historian regarded Justinian as the real ruler of the empire under his uncle Justin, and he attributed to him the misfortunes of that reign as well as of his own. Justin became emperor in 518. If we count thirty-two full years from that date, we reach 550, when Procopius was giving the finishing touches to the seven books of the *History of the Wars,* but before they were finally published. The case for this earlier date was put strongly by one of the foremost scholars of Procopius in the late nineteenth century, and since then, it has been generally accepted.[78]

But this date of 550 for the *Secret History* presents us with a new set of problems. One is that Procopius would have lived on for at least ten more years after he had composed this libelous little document; and yet, like the *Buildings* it betrays signs of being unfinished. A more serious objection is that the evidence of which this date is based is not quite as secure as it seems to be at first glance. No doubt Procopius is writing from the point of view of a man who had witnessed thirty-two years of maladministration under Justin and Justinian, but he had an artistic motive for doing so. The *Secret*

History was intended as a commentary on his major work, the *History of the Wars.* It purported to give causes for events which had to be left out of the published *History* because it was too dangerous to include them. If Procopius could pretend that the *Wars* and the *Secret History* were contemporary, it lent extra force to his claim. But was the pretense based on fact, or was it simply a literary device?

There is one clue which leads me to believe that it was only a literary device. In the *Secret History,* Procopius promises to describe a flood on the river Scirtus in a forthcoming work, and in the *Buildings,* the promise is kept.[79] As we have seen, the *Buildings* was written probably between 558 and 560 at the command of the emperor. If Procopius could refer to it as early as 550, then it meant that he had already received his commission from the emperor at least eight years before he carried it out. One wonders what excuses he gave for postponing his commission so long. It is much more likely that, if Procopius could make a specific cross-reference to the *Buildings* in the *Secret History,* the works were written at about the same time.

If Procopius wrote the *Secret History* at the same time as he was writing the *Buildings,* we may guess his motives. There can be little doubt that he wrote the *Buildings* with some bitterness in his heart. He may have had little choice. The critical tone of the eighth book of the *Wars,* which had just been published, may have caused displeasure. The emperor's suggestion that he compose a eulogistic account of his building program may have had threatening overtones. But while Procopius worked on the frigid praises in the *Buildings,* he poured out his hatred in the *Secret History,* which he wrote for his personal satisfaction. In the *Buildings,* he depicted Justinian as the vicegerent of God, with all the conventional virtues of a Byzantine emperor. In the *Secret History,* we have the opposite picture; Justinian is the prince of the devils. At the end of his career, Procopius looked back on the age with very nearly a schizophrenic vision. The public Procopius carried on as before, concealing his feelings and apparently enjoying some degree of imperial favor. The private Procopius put all his bitterness into a secret pamphlet intended to show that his great work on the wars of Justinian should be reinterpreted in the light of the weakness of Belisarius, the villainy of Antonina his wife, and the superhuman wickedness of Justinian and Theodora.

CHAPTER 2

The History of the Wars of Justinian

I *Books 1 and 2*: The Persian War

IN THE East, the empire faced Persia. By one of the accidents of history, when Justinian ruled at Constantinople, his counterpart in Persia was one of the greatest kings of the Sassanid dynasty, Chosroes Anushirvan ("the blessed"), who figures in Procopius' narrative as a dangerous and faithless villain. Coming to the throne only four years after Justinian and living on to 579, he spent the earlier part of his reign in almost constant war with Byzantium. Armistices punctuated the conflict, but it was not until three years before Justinian's death that a fifty-year peace was signed. It lasted a mere decade, but at least when Justinian died, his eastern frontier was, for the moment, secure.

The dynasty to which Chosroes belonged went back to A.D. 226, when the first Sassanid king, Ardashir, overthrew the royal line of the Parthian Empire, the Arsacids. A few Arsacid princes escaped to Armenia where their descendants continued to rule with Roman support up to the fifth century, but the Sassanids took over the old Parthian realm and established an empire more dangerous to Rome than the Parthians had ever been. The Sassanids were Persians: that is, they belonged to the tribe of the old Achaemenid dynasty which Alexander the Great had overthrown, and they claimed descent from Cyrus and Darius, the founders of the ancient Persian Empire. The pedigree may have been fictitious, but the concept behind it was real enough. If Justinian dreamed of restoring the Roman Empire, Chosroes also had his ambition: to bring back something of the tradition and power of ancient

Persia, which at its height had ruled from India to the Aegean Sea. Like Justinian, who regarded the propagation of orthodox Christianity as a God-given mission, Chosroes actively promoted Zororastrianism, the religion of ancient Persia. Justinian was a reformer; so also was Chosroes. Yet the similarities between the two men only made them more formidable enemies; and in terms of the armed strength which each could muster against the other, they were evenly matched.

Fortunately for Byzantium, the Sassanid dynasty had its weaknesses. The king, *shahanshah,* or "king of kings," was the representation of royal majesty derived from Ahuramazda, supreme god of Zoroastrianism, and in theory his will was law. In practice, however, the priesthood and the great landed magnates severely curtailed his power. In the last analysis, his army depended on the magnates, and no king was ever able to break their strength. As for the Zoroastrian priesthood, the Magi, it became increasingly powerful. The Achaemenids had been Zororastrian, but tolerant of other religions, and the Parthian kings had been half-Hellenized; but under the Sassanids, there was a Zororastrian revival, and the cult became rigid and intolerant. The old permissiveness disappeared, and Christians and Jews were occasionally persecuted. Christians were especially suspect, for Christianity was the official religion of the Roman Empire; and, until the late fifth century, when the church in Persia went over to the Nestorian heresy and effectively broke its ties with the empire, the Persian kings were uncertain of the loyalty of their Christian subjects. The Magi were organized into districts comparable to dioceses, under a supreme Magian or *mobed* who lived at Rhagae. Questions of religious belief were only slightly less important for the Persian kings than they were for the Byzantine emperors.

Procopius begins his narrative of the *Persian War* with an account of Byzantine-Persian relations over the preceding century, and there is some interest in examining his version of events. Emperor Arcadius (d. 408) had requested the king of Persia, one Isdigerdes, to act as guardian of his infant son, who became Theodosius II, and Isdigerdes had accepted this duty and carried it out scrupulously,[1] thus initiating a long period of peace between the two empires which was broken only once. But when Justinian's uncle, Justin, was emperor, Cabades of Persia asked

him to do the same for his heir, Chosroes. Justin and Justinian
were attracted to the idea, Procopius notes, thus diverting any
blame from them. But one of his ministers spoke up against it,
and, misled by this advice, Justin returned an insulting answer.[2]
The implication is that the emperor had blundered unnecessarily
into war by acting less generously than Persia had once done in a
similar situation, although naturally, Procopius allows his readers
to make this inference for themselves. The facts are somewhat
different.

By happy coincidence, in the fifth century when the Roman
Empire in the West broke up and the empire in the East narrowly escaped the same fate, the Sassanid dynasty was passing
through a period of weakness. Yazdegerd I (399-420), the chival-
rous Isdegerdes of Procopius, whom the emperor Arcadius asked
to act as guardian for his infant son, tried to curb the landed
magnates and free himself from the Magi. Consequently, Persian
tradition knew him as "Yazdegerd the Sinner," and his successor,
Bahram Gor, managed to secure the throne only by promising to
reverse his father's policies. The next king, Yazdegerd II (438-
57), had to face a new threat. The Ephthalites or White Huns,
who appeared on Persia's northeastern frontier, occupied the
former Kushan territory in modern Afghanistan and penetrated
into India. The White Huns, to be distinguished from the western
or Black Huns who invaded Europe under Attila, were a mysterious people whose language seems to have been related to
Turkish. But whatever their antecedents, they occupied the energies of the Sassanid kings, and relations with the Roman Empire
remained peaceful until 502.

At that date, the king was Cabades, and it was his relations with
the Huns which led indirectly to the war with Rome. Early in his
reign, he appears to have been inclined toward the Mazdakite
movement, named after its founder Mazdak, who taught a revolutionary social and religious doctrine, which demanded that the
nobles curb their luxury and distribute their surplus wealth to
the poor. The Mazdakites also advocated sharing wives, and it is
this feature alone of their program which Procopius mentions.[3]

As far as Cabades was concerned, he saw the Mazdakites as
potential allies against the all-powerful nobles and Magi. The
movement reached its height between 501 and 523. At the latter

date, Cabades, discovering that the Mazdakite leaders were plotting against him, invited them to a ceremony and there massacred them. By then, his own power was firmly established. But earlier in his reign, his support of the Mazdakites had provoked a rebellion among the nobles, who deposed him and shut him up in the "Castle of Oblivion." It was only with the support of the White Huns that he managed to regain his throne in 501. With Hun assistance, he suppressed the rebels and put out the eyes of an uncle who had ruled during his deposition.

The Huns had to be paid for their help, and Cabades' first interest in the Byzantine Empire was as a source of wealth with which to pay them. He first demanded a loan from the emperor Anastasius, and when Anastasius would not grant it, he launched a raid against imperial territory. But renewed trouble with the Huns made him willing to accept peace with Byzantium a couple of years later, and for the next decade, the Huns kept Cabades fully occupied, until he defeated them at last in 513. Meanwhile, Anastasius seized this opportunity to fortify the cities of Daras in northern Mesopotamia and Theodosiopolis in Armenia. Both were potential threats to Persia, but for the moment, Cabades could do nothing.

War between the two powers broke out again in 527. The cause which Procopius assigned to the outbreak, as we have seen, was Justin's refusal to adopt Cabades' son, Chosroes, in order to secure his succession to the throne of Persia. However, the real reason seems to have been the conflicting religious and territorial ambitions of Byzantium and Persia in the area between the Black and the Caspian seas, the regions now known as Georgia, Transcaucasia, and Azerbaijan. In the western part of this area were the Lazi; next to them the Iberians, and in the eastern part were the Albanians. Lazica was nominally subject to Byzantium, and Iheria rather less nominally to Persia, although the Iberians were Christians. Shortly before 527, Cabades had attempted to force them to accept Zororastrianism, with the result that the Iberian king fled to Lazica and appealed to the emperor Justin. The war that followed was fought on a wide front, and it is with 527 that Procopius takes up the story in detail.

Peace was signed five years later. Both Persia and Byzantium wanted it, Persia because Chosroes had just ascended the throne but was not entirely secure on it, and Justinian because he wanted his hands free to launch an attack on the Vandals. The treaty was called the "Endless Peace." To Procopius' intense indignation, however, Chosroes broke the treaty in 540 and launched an attack on imperial territory, which caused much suffering. In the first two books of the *History of the Wars,* Procopius takes the narrative down to 549 (there was an armistice in 545, but hostilities continued in Lazica); and in the eighth book, he carried it on to 552, after which we are left with the less competent Agathias as our chief source for the Persian War. For the peace treaty which ended the war, we must turn to the fragments of Menander Protector.

II   *The Plan and Method of the* Persian War

When Thucydides wrote his history of the Peloponnesian War, he began with an introduction stating his purpose and his belief that he was writing about the greatest conflict up to his own time, not excepting the war against Troy. To prove his point, he followed this with the so-called Archaeology, a section in which he dissected the evidence from archaic Greece to prove his point. Later, when he came to describe the preliminaries which led to the Peloponnesian War, he traced the history of fifty years of tension between the two power blocs of classical Greece in a separate section called the "Pentekontaetia." The plan may have served Thucydides well, but later scholars were not so certain. In a heavy-handed essay written some five hundred years before Procopius, the rhetorician Dionysius of Halicarnassus observed that Thucydides had erred in separating the "Archaeology" and "Pentekontaetia." He should have begun by tracing the history of Greece from the remote past to the present and then proceeded with his subject.

The secular historians of the late empire were well warned. Ammianus Marcellinus, who contributed greatly to the traditions of the genre, started with Emperor Nerva in A.D. 96, and lightly sketched the history of Rome to his own time, where he took up the story in detail. So also Procopius. He sketches the history of Roman-Persian relations from the death of Arcadius in 408, down to 527, when he was appointed to Belisarius' staff at Daras,

and the main body of his history begins. Both the *Vandal War*
and the *Gothic War* are prefaced by similar sections, which serve
to entertain as well as to give the background; these are places
where edifying or amusing anecdotes can be included for the
reader's delectation. They may also contain implicit comment on
imperial policies. As we have seen, the preface to the *Persian War*
suggested that hostilities broke out in 527 because of a diplo-
matic blunder which the Byzantine Empire might have avoided
had it been better guided.

From 527, Procopius proceeds in detail. About half the first
book treats events down to 532 on the eastern front. This section
falls roughly into two parts, the first revolving around Belisarius'
victory at Daras, which made his reputation, and the second
centering about his defeat the following year at Callinicum. The
one is balanced against the other. Belisarius was recalled after
Callinicum, but Procopius chooses this point to digress on Justinian's relations with the Christian Homeritae, who inhabited the
Yemen. He thus passes over the circumstances of Belisarius' recall
very lightly. Neglecting to mention that Justinian set up a special
commission to investigate the defeat, he moves on to describe the
negotiations for the "Endless Peace."

Most of the remainder of the first book is taken up with two
carefully balanced accounts of domestic sedition in Persia and
in Constantinople. First, Procopius describes two plots against
Chosroes; they are unimportant, although they do serve to put
the king in a bad light. The real reason that Procopius dwells on
the plots is artistic. They serve to balance the Nika rebellion,[4]
which broke out against Justinian in January of 532.

Procopius' account of this revolt is fairly matter-of-fact. In
setting it off against the two plots in Persia, he actually downgrades
the importance of the revolt to some extent, though, in fact, it
nearly ended Justinian's reign. Both factions in the Hippodrome,
the Blues and the Greens, united against the emperor, and he
would have fled with his court had it not been for the courage of
the empress Theodora. As it was, the generals Belisarius and Mundus
with a few soldiers succeeded in massacring the rebels in the
Hippodrome. "And there died among the populace that day,"
wrote Procopius, "more than thirty thousand."[5]

The first book concludes with two digressions. One, at the very end, is a notice of a short-lived mutiny among the troops at Daras. The other deals with the fate of Justinian's praetorian prefect, John the Cappadocian, a rapacious but able man, who although dismissed by the emperor during the Nika revolt to placate the mob, was reappointed by him to his old post after the danger was past. But the empress was John's bitter enemy; thanks to her machinations, he fell in 541, and Procopius chooses to insert the story of his fall here. The passage concludes with the moral comment, "Thus vengeance for his political career overtook John the Cappadocian ten years afterwards"—that is, ten years after the Nika revolt, when John was transported to Egypt and reduced to beggary. Procopius returns again to John's fate at the end of the second book. He tells us that the emperor recalled John to the capital after Theodora died, but he could not recover his position.

In the second book, Procopius leaps forward to the outbreak of hostilities in 540: "Not much later, Chosroes, learning that Belisarius had begun to win Italy too for the Emperor Justinian, no longer could keep his mind in check, but wanted to think up pretexts so as to break the peace treaty on some plausible grounds."[6] Procopius deals with the pretexts first: friction between two Arab tribes in the desert no-man's-land between the empires, one backed by Persia and the other by Byzantium; the urgings of the Gothic king Wittigis, who was hard pressed in Italy and wanted Chosroes to open a second front; and appeals from Armenia. Yet Chosroes' real motive was envy. Procopius digresses briefly to record the appearance of a comet and a new invasion of Huns, but his focus is on Persia. In the spring of 540, as the thirteenth year of Justinian's reign drew to a close, a large Persian army invaded Byzantine territory.

Procopius describes the events season by season (the years are dated at the end of each winter by Justinian's regnal year) up to the truce of 545, and we can sense a new feeling of injury, which was absent in the first book. In particular, there is rising indignation in the description of Chosroes' campaign of 540, which culminated in the sack of Antioch, and it is directed not merely at the unscrupulous king, but in a small way, at God Himself. In 541, Chosroes marched into Lazica and captured the stronghold of Petra on the Black Sea, while back in Mesopotamia, Belisarius again took command and advanced into Persian territory. He bypassed the strong city of Nisibis, but captured Sisauranon, and then beat a retreat. Next year, Chosroes prepared to lead an army across the Euphrates River. Justinian dispatched Belisarius back to the frontier, this time without an army. Even so, Belisarius succeeded by a ruse in discouraging Chosroes from advancing.

Probably no soldiers could be spared, for by then bubonic plague was raging in Constantinople. Procopius seizes the opportunity to describe the plague in a manner intended to recall Thucydides. The plague had begun in Egypt in 541, moved into Palestine, and "from there it fell upon the whole world," reaching Constantinople in mid-spring, 542.[7] The plague at least led Chosroes to abandon the offensive the next year, but in 544 he made an unsuccessful attempt against Edessa, a city which was under the special protection of God, for it possessed a letter written by Christ himself. For religious reasons, Chosroes wished to capture Edessa. The armistice was signed the following year.

By now, the faithlessness of the Persian king had become a background theme. "For," writes Procopius, "soon it became clear that Chosroes had made the peace with treacherous intent."[8] In the third year of the truce, Chosroes made an attempt to capture Daras, but failed.[9] Then he turned to Lazica, and the king of the Lazi, who had been earnestly trying to play off Persia against Byzantium, appealed to Justinian for help. Justinian, delighted to receive the appeal, sent a young general, Dagisthaeus, with seven thousand imperial troops and one thousand allies. Procopius makes a waspish comment on Dagisthaeus' competence, influenced, perhaps, by the fact that Dagisthaeus was under arrest at the time Procopius was composing this passage.[10] Dagisthaeus laid siege to the fortress of Petra, but he handled operations badly and had to withdraw.[11] Nevertheless, the campaign ended with a Roman success.

But this was not quite the end. To balance the digression on John the Cappadocian, which came at the end of the first book, Procopius returns again briefly to the fate of John. This is a grace note borrowed from Herodotus: a digression on which to conclude the serious narrative, and it served also to disguise the fact that Procopius ends the *Persian War* quite arbitrarily. The struggle in the Caucasus region was still going on.

Some six years later, when Procopius continued the history of the *Persian War* in his eighth book, the scene was still Lazica. Rather strangely, he chose this point to insert a geographical description of the area, which gives rise to a number of learned digressions. From the Lazi, he moves on to deal with the various tribes of Huns, whom he identifies with the classical Cimmerians.[12] Then he launches into a scholarly disquisition on the boundaries of Europe and Asia, making an impressive display of his knowledge, with quotations from Herodotus, the *Prometheus Bound* of Aeschylus, and Aristotle,[13] with whom one suspects he was not profoundly acquainted. This last book has more of the smell of the library about it; even if we did not already know it on other grounds, we would have suspected that its author had ceased to be a man of action.

At last, Procopius returns to the war in Lazica and outlines the events down to 552. Dagisthaeus was recalled and imprisoned. His replacement, Bessas, a septagenarian officer whom Procopius had attacked earlier for his misconduct in Italy,[14] recovered Petra; but then, by his inaction, he virtually surrendered Lazica to the Persians. A truce was signed in 552.

Procopius thought this armistice was disastrous for the Byzantines, and he made no secret of it.[15] In fact, compared to his earlier books on the *Persian War*, book eight betrays an altered viewpoint. It is not merely that Procopius is more critical; there was some criticism in the earlier books as well. But his criticism here is more that of an independent observer, a commentator surveying the conduct of the war with an impartial eye. His own personal involvement is a thing of the past.

III   *The Personalities of the* Persian War

Belisarius began his brilliant career just before the death of Emperor Justin, and Procopius notes his debut in history almost casually: "And the Romans under the leadership of Sittas and Belisarius, invaded Persarmenia, a territory subject to the Persians, and laid waste a great area and withdrew with a large number of Armenian captives. And these men were both youths, wearing their first beards, bodyguards of the general Justinian who afterwards shared the empire with his uncle Justin."[16] Sittas was to die young in the emperor's service, but Belisarius went on to

make his reputation by defeating a superior Persian force at
Daras in 530.

Procopius' description of the victory at Daras, and Belisarius'
defeat the next year at Callinicum, dominate the first half of
Book I of the *Wars*. These are almost textbook descriptions, carefully modeled on Thucydides. Yet, there is an immediacy to both,
which indicates that Procopius had his original notes before him
as he wrote. For he must have made notes at the time, not because
he had already decided to write a history, but because, as Belisarius' secretary, he was responsible for drawing up an official
account of these battles. Both these engagements were important
for Belisarius' career: the first displayed his ability, and the second probably prompted his recall to Constantinople. It is worth
examining Procopius' treatment of these accounts.

One could argue that Procopius has given the battle of Daras
more prominence than it deserved. Except for this, his account is
straightforward. Far from raising a paean of praise for his own
commander, Belisarius, he makes it clear that he shared responsibility with the *magister militum* Hermogenes, whom Justinian had
just dispatched to the East. The numbers of the opposing armies
are given: twenty-five thousand Romans and forty thousand Persians; a few paragraphs later, Procopius adds that ten thousand
men joined the Persian army the day after it reached Daras. But
he does not labor the point that the Romans were outnumbered
two to one. The Persian and Roman commanders delivered
speeches to their respective armies before the battle in accordance
with historiographical convention. These speeches are worth examination, for they served as useful devices to convey ideas which
the historian wished to impress on his readers.[17] The Persian
general remarked on the unusual discipline of the Roman army.
However, he added that "if the battle comes to close quarters,
panic and inexperience will seize them, and very likely they will
fall into disorder as usual."[18] Belisarius and Hermogenes spoke
briefly on the same theme from a different viewpoint: the Roman
forces had been defeated in the past because they had not heeded
their officers. If they obeyed commands now, they would win, for
the Persians were basing their hopes for victory on the well-
known indiscipline of the Roman rank and file.[19]

The battle which followed was a splendid example of disciplined maneuvering. In the end, it was the Persians who fled in disarray. Even so, Belisarius and Hermogenes checked any head-long pursuit which might have led to disorder in their own army.

If Daras displayed the results of good discipline, Callinicum, the following year, showed what happened when soldiers were insubordinate. On hearing of a Persian invasion in the north, Belisarius moved quickly across the river Euphrates with twenty thousand men. (Later his Arab ally, Arethas, joined him with an unspecified number of followers.) When the Persians learned of Belisarius' advance, they began to retire. Belisarius followed slowly for he wanted to avoid an engagement. At Callinicum, the Persians were on the point of quitting Roman territory without a battle, but the Byzantine soldiers wanted to fight. Belisarius urged his men to allow the enemy to depart peacefully, since they were already in full retreat and there was no need to take risks. "For," he said, "God ever loves to help men in dangers which are neces-sary, not in those they choose for themselves."[20] But the army began to insult its commander—even some officers joined in—and Belisarius gave way.

The battle was fought evenly until the day was two-thirds done, when Belisarius' Arab allies fell back on the right wing, and the rest of the army was soon in full retreat. The Byzantine soldiers had been fasting, for it was the day before Easter, and they were already exhausted with fighting. There was a contingent of two thousand Isaurians in the army, Procopius reports, and these now fell igno-miniously before the enemy, for they knew nothing about warfare. Yet, these were the very men who had insulted Belisarius most bit-terly before the battle when he had attempted to restrain them.

Belisarius himself held firm as long as he could; then he turned his horse and fled to join his foot soldiers who were still standing their ground. Dismounting, he fought beside them until the day was over. The Persian army departed peacefully the following day, hav-ing suffered no fewer casualties than the Roman force. When the Persian commander reached home, King Cabades did him no honor, but rather rebuked him.

As I have already pointed out, Procopius inserted a digression after Callinicum which took his readers' minds off the consequences of the defeat. He clearly took great pains to have Belisarius emerge blameless, but he avoided eulogy. Belisarius was to occupy center

stage in the *History of the Wars,* and he received many implied
compliments, as well as a few which were openly expressed. But the
ideal of the secular historian was to tell the truth, and the evidence
suggests that Procopius remained as faithful to the ideal as the times
and circumstances permitted.

Rather, his bias was that of an experienced soldier, which he was,
although his usual post was behind a desk in the commander's office.
He saw the battles of Daras and Callinicum as illustrations of the
value of good discipline in the army. The Roman soldiers were victorious when they obeyed their commanders, and when the officers
worked together in harmony, but when they were insubordinate, as
at Callinicum, the result was disastrous. Procopius saw the campaigns
which he described through the eyes of the chiefs of staff. He valued
the military virtues and had only disgust for the civilian bureaucracy,
which was engaged in such pursuits as collecting taxes.

Yet Procopius maintains a judicious tone as he relates the deeds
of Belisarius from 527 to 531. Belisarius was recalled after Callinicum "having been removed from the post which he held, so that
he might march against the Vandals." If this was not the whole
truth, it was at least most of it.

Belisarius returned to the Persian front in 541, and at this point,
if we are to take Procopius' later testimony in the *Secret History*
seriously, he did edit his narrative in Belisarius' favor. For the
Secret History[21] states that Belisarius advanced into Persian territory,
captured the fortress of Sisauranon, and then, hearing that his wife
Antonina was coming, threw away a chance of victory and hurried
back to meet her. In the *Persian War,*[22] Procopius had it that Belisarius retreated for two good military reasons: first, that many of his
soldiers were sick, and second, that he suspected treachery because
he had dispatched the Arab *phylarch* Arethas on a mission from
which he did not return. Procopius does not indicate in the *Secret
History* that his earlier account was untrue; rather he stresses that, in
addition to the strategic reasons for retreat, Belisarius also had a
personal motive. He goes on to imply that this was the real reason
for Belisarius' action. "And yet, if he had been willing to cross the
Tigris River at the beginning with all his army, I think he would
have laid waste the whole land of Assyria, and come right up to the
city of Ctesiphon without meeting any opposition at all; he would
have saved all the prisoners from Antioch and all the other Romans

who happened to be there too, and come back with them to his own country."[23]

Gibbon's comment on this passage is to caution his reader to close his ears to the "malevolent whisper of the *Anekdota*," and his advice is sound. It is not that the *Secret History* lies; on the contrary, its version of Belisarius' retreat is probably built around a kernel of truth. But the secret historian was addicted to the paranoic view of history, where everyone acts from selfish personal motives, and other historical causes have no place. It is worth noting in passing that this view seems to grow on Procopius within the *History of the Wars* itself. For instance, in the *Persian War* he gives three sound geopolitical and strategic reasons why the Persians wanted to control Lazica on the Black Sea.[24] But later, in his eighth book, he adds a purely personal reason. The Persians were dissatisfied with their king Chosroes; consequently, he pressed the attack in Lazica for a self-interested motive: to recoup his prestige by winning a victory there.[25]

Belisarius' last appearance on the Persian front was in 542, when bubonic plague was raging in Constantinople. With a small force he checked Chosroes' advance by an elaborate bluff. Here Procopius praises Belisarius openly. The Persian envoy who came to Belisarius' camp reported back that he "had met a general who was the bravest and the cleverest of all men, and soldiers the like of whom he, at least, had never seen. . . ."[26] The smallness of the Roman army and the vastness of the Persian host are emphasized; Procopius' statistics are vague, but the Persians are numbered in myriads, and the Byzantine force is tiny and in abject terror.[27] Yet, Belisarius achieved his objective, and made Chosroes withdraw. "And the Romans were loud in their praises of Belisarius. . . . For indeed it was an important deed worthy of great praise, that when all the Romans were hiding terrified behind their defenses, and Chosroes with a great army was in the midst of the Roman Empire, a general with a few men should come from Byzantium . . . and Chosroes should no longer advance onward, but in fact, flee. . . ."[28]

The younger Procopius, not yet embittered, would have believed the praise was merited. Belisarius had displayed the qualities which Procopius admired in military men. He took no unnecessary risks, worked toward limited objectives, planned his tactics carefully, faced danger without losing his head, and above all, maintained discipline.

The idealization of Belisarius centers around these virtues, all of them, I suspect, more likely to be admired by a professional soldier than by a civilian. Yet there is an implied lesson in the history of Belisarius' successes. His virtues are those which win battles.

The personality which dominates the second book of the *Persian War,* however, is not Belisarius, but Chosroes, king of Persia. Procopius establishes his character early. "Chosroes, son of Cabades, was a man with an unruly mind, and he was strangely fond of innovations."[29] In Procopius' view, a penchant for innovation was one of the most disastrous qualities which a monarch could possess.[30] One of Chosroes' first acts when he became king was to suppress all opposition. As Procopius handles the story, he was cruel and treacherous to friend and foe alike. This was the man who was filled with envy when he learned of Justinian's victories in the West, and he was determined to break the "Endless Peace" which he had signed in 532. He soon found pretexts for what he wanted to do, but whether these pretexts were true or not, Procopius could not say.[31] In any case, the force which drove him on was jealousy.[32]

Thus, in 540, Chosroes invaded the empire, ravaged the land, and sacked Antioch, a city Procopius must have known well, for its fall clearly made a painful impression on him. Yet behind Chosroes, there was a greater power. A comet had appeared the year before to foretell misfortune,[33] and God had even shown a portent to the Antiochenes, by turning around the standards of the soldiers stationed in the city.[34] It was fated that Antioch should fall.[35] Chosroes emerges as a scourge to whom God, for some reason, had granted permission to inflict harm on the empire. Yet he was an unholy man, an enemy of Christendom, and when in 544, he attacked Edessa, Procopius comments, "Now this invasion was made by this Chosroes, not against Justinian, the emperor of the Romans, but only against the God whom the Christians worship."[36] Without dropping his classical mask, Procopius puts the attack on Edessa entirely within an ideological perspective.

Later, in the *Secret History,* we meet another man whose character presents striking parallels to that of Chosroes in the *Persian War.* It is the emperor Justinian himself.

In the eighth book, Procopius' animus toward Chosroes has not mellowed significantly. He contrasts sharply with the enemies of

Byzantium in the *Vandal* and *Gothic Wars.* The Vandal king Gelimer is a foolish man, but Procopius treats him almost kindly, and he
pays tribute to the good qualities of the Gothic leader, Totila. Chosroes, on the other hand, remains unholy, treacherous, and untrustworthy to the end.

IV   *Books 3 and 4:* The Vandal War

"This, then, was the conclusion of the Persian War for the emperor Justinian," wrote Procopius, by way of introducing his next
topic, and rather overstating the facts, for hostilities in Lazica had
by no means ended. "I shall now go on to describe all that he did
against the Vandals and the Moors. And first I shall tell where the
host of Vandals came from, when they fell upon the land of the
Romans." Forthwith, Procopius plunges into the early history of the
Vandals and tells how they invaded the empire.

This chapter corresponds with the introductory section of the
Persian War, and both begin about the same date: with the death of
Arcadius in the *Persian War,* and with the reign of Arcadius' brother
and co-emperor, Honorius, in the *Vandal War.* First, we have an
essay on geography,[37] which serves to explain how the empire was
divided into eastern and western halves, each with its own emperor.
Then Procopius proceeds, "While Honorius held the imperial power
in the west, the barbarians took over his land."[38]

With this, the story of the barbarian invasions begins, and the
background information provided here is intended not only to put
the Vandals in their proper historical setting, but the Ostrogoths as
well. When we reach the *Gothic War,* Procopius avoids repeating
himself. The history of the Vandal invasion is, briefly, this: In 409,
hordes of Vandals, Sueves, and Alans who had been plundering
Gaul, broke through the Pyrenees, and entered Spain. Up to this
time, Africa had escaped invasion, but in 527, the military commander of Africa, Boniface, was suspected of disloyalty and recalled.
He refused to obey, and the regent Galla Placidia, the mother of the
child-emperor, Valentinian III, sent two expeditions against him,
the second of which had some success. But one tribe of the Vandals
under Gaiseric, seized this opportunity to cross from Spain to Africa,
and Galla Placidia hastily pardoned Boniface so that the Roman

forces might present a united front. It was too late. In 439, Gaiseric took Carthage. Three years later, Rome made peace and recognized the Vandal occupation of much of modern Morocco and Tunisia.

The Vandals were Arians, and unlike most of the other Arian barbarians, they persecuted the Catholics. Gaiseric seized churches and church property and exiled numerous bishops. His son Huneric was even more aggressive. During his brief reign, he exiled the great bulk of Catholic bishops from Africa; many were sent to Corsica, where they were put to work felling timber for the Vandal fleet. The next king, Gundamund, allowed the persecution to lapse, although Procopius avers to the contrary, that he subjected Christians to still greater suffering. His successor, Trasamund, as Procopius states correctly enough, continued the persecution, but by more subtle means. Ilderic, who followed, was an old man, "harsh neither to the Christians nor to anyone else,"[39] and he maintained good relations with Justinian. It was his deposition by Gelimer in 530 which provided the *casus belli*.

Like the introduction to the *Persian War,* this section describing how the Vandals won Africa is told with digressions which are meant to entertain, but they are less innocent than they appear to be on the surface. The story of how the Vandals first entered Africa is an illustration. There were two Roman generals, Boniface and Aetius, both excellent men, and deserving the title, "the last of the Romans."[40] Galla Placidia appointed Boniface to command Africa, which did not at all please Aetius. Consequently, he informed Placidia that Boniface was planning treason, alleging as proof that, if she were to summon him to Rome, he would refuse to come. At the same time, he wrote Boniface that Placidia was plotting against him, and as proof predicted that she would soon summon him to Rome for no good reason. Thus, when the summons came, Boniface was convinced that Aetius had spoken the truth and would not obey; instead he invited the Vandals to invade the province.

This is romanticized history, and Procopius draws no parallels with events of his own day. Yet, there was a parallel: after Belisarius had won Africa, some of his officers spread rumors that he was plotting treason. Justinian gave Belisarius his choice: he could remain in Africa or he could return with his spoils to Constantinople. Belisarius knew of the rumors and knew also that Justinian was aware of them; wiser and more faithful than Boniface, he chose to return to Constantinople. In both instances, the suspicions of treason were groundless.[41]

Another story describes the expedition which Emperor Leo sent from Constantinople against the Vandals, the memory of which was still painfully fresh in Procopius' day.[42] Leo gathered an army reputedly of a hundred thousand men and a fleet from the whole of the eastern Mediterranean, which he put in command of his brother-in-law, Basiliscus. Procopius is uncertain whether this general's incompetence arose from treachery or simple cowardice; in any case, Basiliscus allowed his fleet to be destroyed by Vandal fire ships, and he accomplished nothing. Procopius leaves it to the reader to draw the parallel with Belisarius' expedition, which was of modest size but disembarked on the coast of Africa before the Vandals guessed the danger and proceeded with the conquest speedily and efficiently.

Thus the tone is set for the central narrative of the *Vandal War*: the victorious expedition of Belisarius, which, happily, has a beginning, middle, and end. To open it, Procopius describes a scene which closely parallels one described by Herodotus a thousand years earlier. In order to announce the expedition he planned to make against Greece in 480 B.C., Xerxes summoned his satraps, who listened to the king in silence. They disapproved of his plan but were afraid to speak out, until the king's uncle, Artabanus, finally voiced an objection.[43] Likewise, in the council of imperial officials which Justinian summoned to announce his Vandal expedition, everyone was filled with foreboding. The man who filled the role of Artabanus was the praetorian prefect, John the Cappadocian, whose subsequent disgrace and punishment had already provided Procopius with artistic conclusions for both books of the Persian War. Here he is called "a man of greatest boldness and the cleverest of all men of his own time,"[44] and the speech he delivered convinced the emperor against the expedition, just as Artabanus had convinced Xerxes.

Then there appeared on the scene "a certain one of the priests whom they call bishops."[45] He had come from the East, roused by a dream in which God had commanded him to rebuke Justinian for abandoning the Christians in Libya to their Vandal oppressors. " 'And yet,' He had said (so the bishop reported) "if he goes to war, I Myself will help him and make him lord of Libya.' " Thereupon the emperor "could no longer restrain his purpose."[46] In the sequel, the Christian God proved a trustworthy ally. In Herodotus, Xerxes too had been persuaded by a dream, but the dream proved delusive.

There follows a brief section on the situation in Libya (Gelimer faced revolts in Tripolis and Sardinia) and the mustering of the Byzantine armada. It ends with a strange tale of foreboding: Justinian sent a detachment of the fleet in advance to await the main force in the Peloponnesus. As it was setting sail, he remembered something he had forgotten to mention to the two commanders, Martinus and Valerian. So he summoned them back; then, changing his mind, he sent messengers to countermand his order. The sight of these men shouting to the departing vessels not to return struck bystanders as an ill omen, though, as it turned out, no curse fell on Martinus or Valerian. But among their bodyguards was Stotzas, who would lead a mutiny later in Libya, and, remarks Procopius, "one might suspect that the curse was turned on him by Heaven. But whether this matter can be explained this way or some other, I leave each one to reason as he wishes. But I shall go on to tell how the general Belisarius, and the army departed."[47]

The armada set sail with the blessing of the patriarch in 533 A.D., about the time of the summer solstice. At Abydos, where the fleet was becalmed for four days, Belisarius made an example of two Huns[48] in his army who had murdered a comrade while they were drunk. He crucified them and seized the occasion to deliver a homily on drunkenness and violence. Here was a commander who enforced discipline and would not tolerate insubordination; the virtues of which Procopius approves are in full display.

From Abydos, the expedition sailed across the Aegean and around the Peloponnesus to Methone. There it was laid low by an epidemic (probably ptomaine poisoning) caused by the rotten bread with which John the Cappadocian had supplied it. Belisarius secured local supplies for his men and reported the situation to the emperor. Then it proceeded on to Sicily, where all the drinking water on the fleet spoiled, except on the flagship, where Belisarius' wife, Antonia, had preserved it by storing it in glass jars buried in sand. "So much, then, for this," concludes Procopius, and turns to what happened in Sicily.

At this point, Procopius appears in the narrative himself, acting as Belisarius' right-hand man. He tells the story with some pride. Dispatched to Syracuse to garner information, he brought back word that the Vandals were completely unsuspecting, and this news cheered the soldiers, who had been afraid of encountering the Vandal fleet. The armada touched Africa at Caput Vada (Shoal's Head) and disembarked there, five days' journey from Carthage "for an unencumbered man."[49]

Before disembarkation, Belisarius called his officers together on his flagship and held a debate on the course of action to take.[50] This is an artfully contrived scene, for although Belisarius could have held a council of his officers, and probably did, it could hardly have taken the form reported here, which is designed to allow Belisarius room to explain his plan of attack, and, incidentally, to display his strategic abilities. Archelaus, the officer in charge of supplies and maintenance, spoke first, and urged a direct attack on Carthage itself. Then Belisarius set forth the advantages of disembarking at Caput Vada: in this way, they avoided the perils of a naval encounter and of bad weather and took best advantage of the element of surprise. Anyone familiar with Thucydides would be conscious of a latent comparison with the ill-fated Athenian expedition to Sicily which he chronicled:[51] here, in contrast to the Sicilian expedition, where there were three generals and three strategies, there is a single able commander with a prudent plan of attack.

After disembarkation, Procopius strikes another familiar note, the importance of discipline. Belisarius kept his soldiers in order and would not allow them to plunder the farmers' crops, for this would alienate the Libyan populace.[52] Later, before entering Carthage, Belisarius was to remind his men once again of the value of self-control. "For all the Libyans had been Romans in past time, and not of their will had they become Vandal subjects and suffered many outrages from these barbarians."[53] Indeed, the war was to be directed not against the Libyans, or even the Vandals, but specifically against Gelimer, whom Justinian regarded as a usurper.

Belisarius won his first victory at Decimum (the tenth milestone from Carthage), and afterward the imperial forces entered Carthage, where Belisarius and his officers, including Procopius, entered the royal palace, and ate a meal there which had been prepared for Gelimer the day before. But the Vandal king still had support in the countryside among the native population, and his brother, Tzazon, who had just crushed a rebellion in Sardinia, hurried back to help as soon as he heard of the defeat at Decimum. About mid-December, 533, there was a second battle at Tricamaron, slightly less than twenty miles from Carthage, and it was another victory for Belisarius. Tzazon was killed; Gelimer fled to Mount Papua in Numidia where he was ultimately starved into surrender and taken to Constantinople. Procopius sums it up: "I cannot say if deeds like these have ever happened before, that the fourth descendant of Gaiseric and his realm, which was at the height of its wealth and military strength, were overthrown in so short a time by five thousand men, coming as invaders, and without a harbour. For this was the number of cavalry which followed Belisarius, and carried through the whole war against the Vandals. One would rightly marvel at this, whether it happened by chance or by some kind of valor. . . . So the Vandal war ended thus."[54]

However, the war was followed by a revolt of the Moors and a mutiny of the army, which narrative takes up the better part of the second book. First, Procopius relates how Belisarius returned to Constantinople under circumstances which offered a close parallel to the story of Boniface and Galla Placidia, related in his introductory section. Some of Belisarius' officers slandered him to the emperor. Justinian gave no indication whether or not he believed the slanders, but he gave Belisarius his choice, either to return home with Gelimer and the other Vandal captives, or else to send along the captives and stay behind in Africa himself. Belisarius, who was well aware of what his officers had done, chose to return. It is abundantly clear what Procopius' opinion of the matter was: had Belisarius remained in charge, the revolt of the Moors would never have occurred, for they were overawed by his military prestige.[55]

These Moors, as Procopius explains in an excursus which shows a good knowledge of the Bible, were descendants of the Canaanites who were driven from Palestine by Joshua, the son of Nun, and he reports that up to his own day, they still spoke the Phoenician tongue.[56] Their revolt actually started before Belisarius set sail (Procopius reports this fact even though it does not quite coincide with his view that Belisarius' departure brought about the uprising), but he could not delay. Turning the command over to Solomon, he left for Constantinople.

Before plunging into Solomon's operations against the Moors, Procopius describes the reception which Belisarius received in Constantinople—a celebration he could not have witnessed himself, for it soon transpires that he remained in Africa, attached to Solomon's staff.[57] His account of the Moorish campaign is, therefore, based on firsthand information. So also is the mutiny of the Byzantine army which broke out in 536. However, when Solomon and a few officers fled from Carthage to escape the mutineers, Procopius escaped along with them to Sicily to rejoin Belisarius. Though he may have returned to Africa briefly when Belisarius made an unsuccessful attempt to restore order there, after 536, as far as we know for certain, all his information about Africa was secondhand. Yet, he continued to be well informed.

The mutiny was suppressed at last by the emperor's cousin, Germanus, a general whom Procopius always treats with great respect. Germanus' tactics were an exercise in careful expertise; upon reaching Carthage, he found that two-thirds of the army was on the side of the mutineers. By carefully building up his power base, he eventually won a military advantage. Yet, once the mutiny was suppressed and its leader Stotzas had retired to Mauretania, Justinian recalled Germanus and sent back Solomon.

Procopius has high praise for Solomon. "And under his rule," he wrote, "Libya became a secure source of revenue, and prosperous in other respects."[58] The Moors were defeated; the Libyans enjoyed peace, and were content with Byzantine rule. But a few years later, all this changed. Justinian put two of Solomon's nephews in command of two Libyan cities. One of these, Sergius, *dux* of Tripolitania, whom Procopius characterizes as "exceedingly stupid and immature, both in character and years,"[59] demolished all the blessings of Solomon's rule. He provoked another Moorish uprising, and Solomon was killed in battle. Then, to compound his error, Justinian appointed Sergius to succeed Solomon as governor, and things went from bad to worse.

For practical purposes, the Vandal War ends with 545. One more paragraph, possibly added in the final editing before publication, brings the history of events down to 548. In these years, John of Troglita in a great campaign, which was to be the subject of a not inconsiderable Latin epic by Procopius' contemporary, Corippus, suppressed the Moors and brought peace to Libya. Yet Procopius' final words are deeply pessimistic: "Thus the Libyans who survived, who were few in number and exceedingly poor, at last, after great toil, got some peace."[60]

Procopius inserts only one paragraph on Africa in his eighth book, and it does no more than rephrase the conclusion of the *Vandal War* John of Troglita had incredibly good luck, and peace returned to Libya. "However, "Procopius continues, "because of the earlier wars and rebellions, the land for the most part remained deserted."[61]

The Vandal campaign was a great enterprise, and there were officers of high ability who carried it out. But it was marred by mistakes in imperial policy; and though Procopius does not say so explicitly, by implication, they were the emperor's mistakes. There was one disastrous appointment as governor, again the emperor's misjudgment. In the end, the Byzantines created a desert and called it peace, and the *Vandal War* concludes in a mood tinged with bitterness.

V *Books 5, 6 and 7:* The Gothic War

The *Gothic War* begins with the familiar preface, intended to give the historical background and setting for the main subject. However, the introductory section of the Vandal War had already partially covered the barbarian invasions, and Procopius does not repeat himself. Instead, he begins with Romulus Augustulus, the emperor whose deposition in 476 supplies us with the conventional date for the fall of the empire in the West. He proceeds with a swift description of how the Ostrogoths invaded Italy, but his account remains very sketchy and abbreviated until he reaches the death of Theodoric, the year before Justinian became emperor. By this time, we are already dealing with the preliminaries of Justinian's Gothic War itself.

This preface contains little which is intended simply to entertain the reader. There is also another feature we might not expect: the treatment of the enemy is, on the whole, complimentary. Theodoric never claimed the title of *basileus* (emperor), but continued to be called *rex* (king) to the end of his life, and yet he possessed the qualities with which nature endows a true *basileus*. Procopius makes it clear what these qualities are. Theodoric observed justice, upheld the laws (that is, he was no innovator), protected the land from the foes on its borders, and acted wisely and bravely. He was in name a "tyrant," that is, a man who had usurped power; but in fact, he was as true an emperor as anyone who had held the office.[62]

We may conjecture that one reason for this complimentary treatment of Theodoric is that shortly before the publication of the *Gothic War,* Theodoric's granddaughter had married the emperor's cousin, Germanus, whom Procopius always treats with favor. But more important must have been his own experience in Italy, where he took the measure of the Ostrogoths himself, and learned what sort of reputation Theodoric possessed. We do not know who his informants were. It would be helpful if we knew what friends Procopius made in Italy outside his own military circle, but he gives us no clues by which we can identify them. He must have made contacts with the senatorial class in an official capacity, but they were civilians; he was a soldier, and when he describes[63] their conduct during the siege of Rome in the first winter of the campaign, he shows some of the typical reaction of the soldier to the civilian. He gives no hint of any interest in contemporary Latin literature. He does mention Boethius, the most important Latin author of the sixth century, but he labels him simply a man who practiced philosophy, and his claim to fame is that Theodoric put him to death.[64] I shall suggest later that Procopius may have shared a part of Boethius' philosophic outlook, and there is at least the possibility that he had read Boethius. But the evidence is anything but compelling. Procopius' exact contemporary, Cassiodorus, might not have existed, although he had written a history of the Goths which would have been useful, and certainly it was available. A Goth in Constantinople, Jordanes, published a digest of it just before the *History of the Wars of Justinian* appeared. Evidently, contemporary letters in Italy held no interest for Procopius.

But the past did. Procopius was aware that on every side of him in Italy were relics of the great past which Greece and Rome both shared. In Rome could be seen the ship of Aeneas in its boathouse by the Tiber,[65] and in the temple of Fortune he found a copy of the Palladium which Odysseus and Diomedes had stolen from Troy and noted that it looked more Egyptian than Greek.[66] The Romans of his day, he tells us, loved their city and were anxious to protect her ancestral treasures.[67] What benefit did the Gothic War bring these people? Rome was depopulated and the land stripped. If Procopius looked back on Theodoric's reign with regret, he may simply have reflected the mood of a vast number of Italians.

Theodoric's successor was his little grandson, Atalaric; since he was still a child, his mother Amalasuntha acted as regent. Amalasuntha planned to educate her son as a Roman prince, but the

Gothic leaders insisted that he be brought up according to the customs of his people and forced his mother to give way. But Atalaric's barbarian education rapidly transformed him into a drunkard and a lecher, and Amalasuntha, who felt that she was losing control over her child, made her first overture to Justinian.

Atalaric died in 534 after an eight-year reign, and Amalasuntha (for, writes Procopius, she was fated to fare badly)[68] married her cousin Theodatus, made him king, and informed Justinian of what she had done. But before her messengers reached Constantinople, Theodatus had imprisoned and killed her, thus presenting the emperor with justification for invading Italy.

The Byzantine attack was to come on two fronts. One army, led by Mundus, the commander of Illyricum, would move into Dalmatia, while Belisarius would sail directly against Sicily. At the same time, Justinian sent a letter to the Franks in Gaul, who were Catholics rather than Arians, and might be expected to sympathize with the imperial cause for reasons of religion. Procopius quotes it verbatim. It sets forth succinctly the reasons for the war, as Justinian saw them: "The Goths have forcibly seized Italy, which was ours, and have not only refused to return it, but have done us further injustices which pass all measure, and cannot be endured. Therefore, we are forced to make an expedition against them, and it is proper that you should join us in this war, which is our common interest, both because of the orthodox faith which rejects the belief of the Arians, and because of the hostility we both feel towards the Goths."[69]

The recovery of imperial territory and the orthodox faith were the reasons for the attack. Whether or not this is an authentic letter of Justinian, it sums up well the motives which lay behind his policy.

VI   *The Plan of the* Gothic War

Procopius proceeds with his Gothic War from 535 according to the plan with which we are already familiar, chronicling events year by year, and marking off each year at the end of winter. Thus he ticks off the spring of 536, when Belisarius crossed over to Italy, with, "And the winter ceased, and the first year ended of this war of which Procopius wrote the history."[70]

Yet, within this year-by-year framework, the treatment is uneven.

The first year of the war, when Belisarius conquered Sicily, is dealt with briefly. But the second year was 536-37, when Belisarius moved into Italy, captured Naples, marched north and occupied Rome, and was in turn besieged there by Wittigis, who had replaced the incompetent Theodatus as king. This year takes up only a little less space than the next three years combined. I suspect that part of the reason for this was that the story of the siege of Rome was originally a separate essay written six years or so before the *Gothic War* was published as a whole, and when Procopius fitted it into the continuous narrative of his history, he did not abbreviate it or change it significantly. In any case, the story of this year was filled with stirring events, and Procopius felt that he should relate them in detail.[71]

The sixth book ends with the return of Belisarius to Constantinople in early 540. If the last book of the *Gothic War* had been lost without a trace, I am not sure that scholars would have guessed that Procopius intended to write anything further on the subject. Yet the war in Italy flared up again, and the seventh book continues the narrative of events between 540 and 550. The treatment of the individual years is comparatively thin, possibly because there was nothing stirring to recount, or perhaps simply because Procopius himself was no longer in Italy, and he lacked the detailed information he had had for the earlier years. As I have noted earlier, the twelfth year of the war (546-47) is treated in greater detail. Perhaps Procopius revisited Italy briefly that year, or perhaps the reason is only that he found a garrulous informant. In 548, Belisarius' wife, Antonina, returned to Constantinople, and although the evidence of the *Secret History* indicates that Procopius hated her, he could nevertheless have found her a useful source. After the twelfth year of the war, if we discount digressions, the treatment of events tends to be thin right down to the end of the eighth book.

The *Gothic War* begins with Belisarius occupying center stage, and his great scene is the siege of Rome, when Wittigis shut him up in the supposedly indefensible city for a year and nine days. No other event is treated with such detail. It is a story of skirmishes and battles which possess a Homeric quality, and speeches which debate the rights and wrongs of the war as both sides saw them. Yet, Procopius cannot suppress a slight note of criticism even here. For instance, Belisarius allowed Wittigis to seize the Portus Traiani, the harbor built to serve Rome by the emperor Trajan some two miles

from Ostia, and this made it more difficult to supply the city by sea.
Yet, the historian comments, with even three hundred men, it should
have been possible to hold the Portus.[72] By implication, of course,
this criticism touched Belisarius less than it did Justinian, who was
ultimately responsible for the inadequate army defending Rome.

The odds against Belisarius were staggering. Writing to Justinian
to beg for reinforcements, he stated that he had only five thousand
men, while the enemy numbered one hundred and fifty thousand.[73]
Yet, Procopius points out that not all the advantages were on the
Gothic side. All the Byzantines and their allies were good mounted
bowmen. But the Gothic cavalry fought only with spears and
swords, while their archers fought on foot, and entered battle under
cover of heavily armed men.[74] So long as Belisarius used hit-and-
run tactics, he could hurt the Goths badly without suffering casualties himself, but when he attempted a pitched battle outside the
walls, the end was disastrous. We are not surprised to find that
Belisarius' soldiers demanded this battle, and Belisarius himself con-
sented to it with reluctance. It is the story of Callinicum over again;
a strategic error becomes an illustration of the evils of disobedience.[75]

Even before the siege of Rome was over, there emerges another
theme: discord among the officers, and insubordination. The "envy
of fortune" inspired a quarrel between Belisarius and one of his
officers, Constantinus, over a pair of valuable daggers which
Constantinus had stolen from a civilian.[76] Belisarius demanded that
Constantinus return the daggers to their owner; both officers lost
their tempers, and Constantinus attempted to stab Belisarius. Belisarius' guards seized him and took him away; sometime later,
Belisarius had Constantinus put to death. Procopius comments, "This
was the only unholy deed done by Belisarius, and it was in no way
worthy of his character, for in his treatment of all others, he always
showed great gentleness." However, insubordination was to be a
continuing problem. After the siege was over, John, the nephew of
Vitalian, who had seized Ariminum, refused to obey Belisarius'
command to withdraw.[77] Hence, he found himself beleaguered by
the Goths, for Ariminum lay on their path as they retired from
Rome to Ravenna. Belisarius showed little eagerness to relieve his
officer. About midsummer, 538, the eunuch Narses arrived with
five thousand men. Along with John, who was finally rescued and

emerged from the siege emaciated and hostile to Belisarius, Narses formed an alliance which, in effect, split the Byzantine army in Italy into two separate forces, one commanded by Narses and the other by Belisarius. Procopius' version of what happened implies that it was Narses who was at fault, although the reader who reads between the lines may suspect that Belisarius had acted like a prima donna and was not entirely innocent. The immediate result of this quarrel was that the Goths were able to recapture Milan, which had come over to the emperor earlier. When the city fell, they massacred the male population and enslaved the women.[78] When Justinian learned of this disaster, he recalled Narses, but he punished no one for what had happened, as Procopius reports with, one suspects, covert indignation.[79]

Even so, there was feeling against Belisarius among his officers, and soon it was Belisarius himself who was insubordinate. Chosroes was threatening in the East, and Justinian wanted peace in Italy. But Belisarius was determined on victory, and he sabotaged negotiations.[80] Ultimately, Belisarius took Ravenna by leading the Goths to believe that, if they surrendered to him personally, he would declare himself independent king of Italy. However, once he had taken the Gothic capital, he repudiated all thought of disloyalty to Justinian and departed to Constantinople with Wittigis and the Gothic treasure which he had captured.

The emperor's reception was noticeably reserved. Yet, the fame of Belisarius filled the capital, and at this point in his history, Procopius chooses to insert a eulogy of his old general.[81] When Belisarius commanded an army, soldiers and peasants both loved him: the soldiers because he was generous, consoled them with gifts when they were wounded, and made good their losses; the peasants because he showed restraint and consideration. They were not plundered when Belisarius' army was in the land; instead, they set their own prices for their goods, and the army bought them. Belisarius was a virtuous man who touched no woman except his wife; he was courageous without being foolhardy, and he acted shrewdly in difficult situations. He was neither self-indulgent nor vain, and as a final compliment, Procopius says that no one ever saw him drunk.

The commanders left behind in Italy were very dissimilar. They plundered the natives of Italy, and at the same time, failed to secure the obedience of their soldiers, so that Byzantine power was rapidly destroyed. "These events," writes Procopius, "I shall proceed to narrate as best I can."

On the Byzantine side, events of these years between 540 and 550 are a fabric of mistaken policies and incompetent leadership, and behind the Thucydidean mask which he assumes, Procopius is critical and indignant. The first error was to send out one Alexander as *logothetes,* whose duty it was to put accounts in order and collect revenue. Alexander alienated both the Italians and the Byzantine soldiers by his harshness toward the former and his stinginess toward the latter. Because the soldiers were not paid, they grew insubordinate, and their officers shut themselves up behind the walls of the cities, where they lived with their mistresses and allowed the situation in the countryside to deteriorate. Belisarius was sent back to Italy in 544, but with few troops, and he accomplished little. Procopius makes no effort to conceal Belisarius' failure; he states baldly that Belisarius had succeeded in disembarking nowhere in Italy during the five years he spent there until 549, but had been forced to flit from one fortified coastal town to another, while the Goths remained firmly in control of Italy.[82] Procopius does hint that when Justinian recalled Belisarius in 549, he had him in mind for another command against Persia. Perhaps this was to save face. At any rate, nothing came of it, and Procopius allows the hint to stand without further comment.[83]

At this point, the historian comes close to open criticism of the emperor himself. Had Justinian replaced Belisarius promptly with a vigorous commander, he might have overcome the Goths. But Justinian's interests were absorbed elsewhere; the phraseology of Procopius is delicate but clear. In the eighth book he was to repeat this criticism, but without bothering to veil it. Justinian, he states simply and openly, conducted the war in Italy negligently.[84]

Totila, the Gothic king who rallied the Goths after the surrender of Ravenna, stands in sharp contrast to the Byzantine commanders. He displayed kindness toward his captives[85] and kept his troops under firm discipline. A Roman complained that one of Totila's bodyguards had violated his daughter; Totila executed the guilty man and told the Goths who protested that every man's fortune was decreed according to the conduct of his life. God favored the just, he urged in a remarkable speech which Procopius put into his mouth; there-

fore let the Goths observe justice.[86] Once it was Belisarius whom
Procopius idealized as the embodiment of the virtues with which he
here endows Totila, and they bring him the same success that they
had brought Belisarius. Nothing shows more clearly than the seventh
book of the *Wars* how narrowly Procopius saw military victory in
terms of leadership: the Byzantines lost ground because the soldiers
were undisciplined and their officers unworthy men; the Goths won
because Totila possessed the qualities of a great general. It remained
for a modern historian to show how seriously the Byzantine army
was hampered by the plague which broke out in 541, making reinforcements harder to find than usual.[87] For Procopius, the plague did
not exist as a military factor.

Finally, Justinian appointed a commander of whom Procopius
could approve: his cousin, Germanus. But Germanus died in 550,
without ever reaching Italy, and the *Gothic War* ends on an incon-
clusive note, with Totila in command of most of the peninsula and
Sicily.

Two years later, the Goths were finally crushed by a Byzantine
army led by Narses. These events are narrated in Procopius' eighth
book, but in such a way that Narses received little glory from it. By
design, the history of Narses' campaign is tucked in at the end of the
book, after Procopius has dealt fully with events in Persia and in-
dulged in long digressions on geography and tidbits of barbarian
history. He also takes care to emphasize the importance of a naval
engagement before Narses arrived on the scene, where John, the
nephew of Vitalian, and Valerian defeated the Gothic fleet off
Ancona. Procopius declares that this victory broke the spirit of the
Goths and Totila.[88] Yet, he gives Narses credit for generosity.
Everyone was eager to serve under him.[89] One can catch a trace
of grudging admiration in his account of Narses' conduct before
Justinian, for Narses refused to accept the command in Italy unless
Justinian gave him sufficient money to see that the soldiers were
properly paid.[90]

The Battle of Busta Gallorum, where Totila died and the Ostrogoths were crushed, was a sound piece of strategy, but Belisarius is
careful to point out the odds. They were not five thousand to one
hundred and fifty thousand, as they had been for Belisarius during
the epic days of the first siege of Rome. The Byzantines now had
the larger force, and Procopius emphasizes the fact. Narses, deliver-

ing the conventional speech to his men before the battle, stated baldly: "You, my good fellows, have to fight an enemy vastly inferior to you in courage, numbers and every sort of equipment." All that was necessary, he went on piously, was the help of God. Totila also spoke to his men, who were terrified by the Byzantine army. His was more a speech of desperation; he urged his men to be courageous, and yet, Procopius has him, too, remark on the vast numbers of the enemy.[91]

After Busta Gallorum, the Byzantines recaptured Rome (actually taken by Dagisthaeus, who had earlier been recalled from Lazica and imprisoned) and then crushed the last Gothic resistance at a battle fought at Mons Lactarius near Naples. Here the heroism was all on the side of the Goths, and Procopius singles out the last stand of Teias, who led the Goths after Totila's death, as worthy of comparison with the heroes of legend. After the battle was over, Narses allowed the remnant of the Goths to leave Italy. "And the eighteenth year as it closed," Procopius concludes, "brought to an end this Gothic War of which Procopius has written the history."

CHAPTER 3

The Buildings

No ONE now is likely to read the *Buildings* of Procopius merely for pleasure. Panegyric is one *genre* of literature from the ancient world which has not worn well with time, even though it is a close relative of the modern art of advertising. The chief attraction of the *Buildings* for the scholar now is that it provides a full and remarkably accurate account of Justinian's building program; thanks to it, the architectural history of Justinian's reign is better known than that of any other single emperor.[1] Whatever its failings may be as literature, the *Buildings* is a mine of information.

Procopius wrote this work at the emperor's suggestion, as he indicates himself, for when he comes to describe the churches built in Constantinople, he begins with those dedicated to Mary, the Mother of God, explaining that Justinian himself had wanted him to follow this order.[2] Evidently, when it came to planning the work, Justinian made Procopius aware of his preferences, and this implies that he inspired the *Buildings* in the first place. Professor Glanville Downey has suggested that the first book was written originally as a panegyric to be delivered at court; then, at the emperor's command, Procopius amplified this beginning into six books to cover the building program in the whole empire.[3] Whether this suggestion is true or not, there was only one source where Procopius could have found information as full and accurate as he evidently possessed, and that was in the imperial archives.[4] Very likely, Justinian not only commissioned the *Buildings* but saw to it that Procopius had access to the information necessary to write it.

We may perhaps draw a parallel from an event which one of Procopius' contemporaries, John the Lydian, describes in his own career. John was a civil servant with good literary training and a sound knowledge of Latin; regrettably, both these qualifications,

which were necessary for advancement in the bureaucracy when John
started out, declined in importance under Justinian. A disappointed
man, John retired after forty years of service to devote himself to
literature. However, he does describe one reward which came his
way. He writes: "The emperor, who had learned how I worked day
and night on literature, first invited me to address a panegyric to him
(there happened to be in the audience important people from old
Rome, who always take a deep interest in the study of literature,
even in the midst of their present sufferings). After I had given this
speech, he commissioned me also to do a history of the war against
the Persians. . . . This was the time when they retreated from the
city of Daras . . . which they had been harassing, and made for
home with no small losses. . . ."5

John's history of the Persian War (now lost) was commissioned,
it would appear, to handle Belisarius' victory at Daras in a way
which flattered Justinian. We can only surmise what John said. No
doubt he made Justinian the direct cause of the victory, just as
Procopius makes him directly responsible for all the buildings of
his empire. However, we can guess that Justinian provided Procopius
with the inspiration for the *Buildings* no less directly than he did
John, and perhaps by a similar method.

Facts fail us, but imagination may supply a few details. Procopius
had just published the eighth book of his *History of the Wars,* and
its critical tone was unmistakable. The tenor of the first seven books,
published in 551, can hardly have been entirely pleasing to the
imperial court, but Procopius' genius was apparent to all, and the
emperor recognized literary merit. However, the lack of enthusiasm
was too clear for comfort in the last book, and perhaps the aging
emperor had grown more sensitive to criticism, for in his later years,
he seems to have tried to enlist support from the literati for his
sagging regime. In any case, Procopius, like John the Lydian, may
have received an imperial invitation to deliver a panegyric before
the court; unlike John, he did not welcome it, but he understood
what he was meant to do. With well-concealed bitterness, he composed what later, revised and expanded with the emperor's advice,
became the first book of the *Buildings.* To this, five more books were
added. Yet Procopius had his revenge. As he was working on the
Buildings, he was quietly composing the *Secret History,* which
amounted to a revision of the first seven books of *History of the*

Wars. This was the piece which had made his literary reputation, and the emperor had found it comparatively acceptable. Procopius may have comforted himself that if the emperor could have read what was omitted from those eight books, he would have speedily changed his mind.

It appears from recent research[6] that the *Buildings* was published in two versions. An early one was put in circulation during Procopius' lifetime, and this was followed by a second, partially revised and edited version which was issued after Procopius' death. Yet, even this revised version was unfinished. There is some evidence of carelessness in revision; on one occasion, Procopius describes the same thing twice,[7] and on three occasions he simply gives long, schematic lists of buildings,[8] as if the subject matter had temporarily defeated his literary skill. Possibly, he intended to rework these passages later. One omission, of course, is glaring. Nothing at all is said of Justinian's buildings in Italy.

I   *The Plan*

Procopius' introduction to his eulogy is artful, and it establishes at the beginning the picture of Justinian as the ideal emperor, fulfilling the role for which God had intended him. Subjects who received benefits from their rulers should repay them with thanks, he says, and the benefits bestowed by Justinian were great: he added to the Roman domain, destroyed error in the Christian faith, and set the law in order. Lastly, he provided for the empire's defense with many soldiers and fortresses constructed on the imperial frontiers. Procopius goes back in history and compares Justinian to the Athenian Themistocles, and to Cyrus: not the historical Cyrus who founded the Persian Empire, but the idealized Cyrus, the perfect prince whose education was described in a fictional but influential essay by Xenophon in the fourth century B.C. Procopius manages a weak pun on the title of Xenophon's *Cyropaedeia*[9] and then passes on to the main body of the panegyric. It is worth noting in passing, that twice in this preface, Procopius alludes to his *History of the Wars* with the delicate suggestion that he had actually written that work to the glory of Justinian,[10] an interpretation we might not have guessed by ourselves.

The first book then proceeds to describe buildings constructed or reconstructed in the capital. It was natural to start with Hagia Sophia and perhaps equally natural to continue with constructions close by: the equestrian statue of Justinian, and the church of Hagia Eirene, which still stands in Istanbul. Next, Procopius launches into a new section devoted to Justinian's churches in Constantinople, beginning with those dedicated to the Mother of God. Then come public buildings, a palace, a reservoir and harbor works, but the emphasis of the first book is on the pious Justinian, who built to the glory of God.

The second book shows Justinian in his role as defender of the empire. Starting with the great fortress of Daras, with which Procopius must have been very familiar himself, he proceeds to describe the defense works constructed on the Persian frontier. Indeed, the emperor made Mesopotamia manifestly inaccessible to Persian invasion.[11] (Can there be a trace of irony here?) The third book takes the reader to Armenia. Justinian had conferred complete security on the Armenians; and to their neighbors, the Tzani, he brought the blessings of civilization and Christianity. For the sake of completeness, this book also touches Lazica and the cities on the Black Sea.

The fourth book moves into Europe but confines itself to Greece and the Balkans, omitting Constantinople, which had been the subject of Book I. By this point, the treatise is showing signs of careless composition. The next book returns to Asia and takes up the thread where Book II left off. The second book had enumerated all the cities in the East from the Persian boundary to Palmyra: Book V promises to continue the description of Asia and to pass on to Libya.[12] However, in spite of the promise, it does not go beyond Palestine and ends with a list of monasteries which benefited in some way or other from Justinian's penchant for building, if only by getting a new well. Strangely, the list concludes with some buildings outside Palestine, as if what we have here is only Procopius' working notes, jotted down from some record in the archives and only partially digested. The last book starts with Egypt, moves on to Libya, and ends with brief notices on Sardinia and the Pillars of Hercules.

We might logically expect Italy to be next, but the *Buildings* breaks off abruptly at this point. In fact, both the last two books look as if they had been subjected to some inexpert editing; originally, they may have made up a single book, which was divided arbitrarily into two,[13] probably not by Procopius. It is this last section in particular which leads us to conclude that the *Buildings* is unfinished.

Procopius followed a simple geographical plan, starting off with the capital, then dividing the empire into areas, and undertaking to deal with each one exhaustively. Much of the building he described was routine work, and a good deal of it he must have known only from the imperial archives. However, he concludes with a weak echo of Thucydides, claiming that he had written about buildings which he had seen himself, or heard described by others who had seen them.[14] It is by no means a completely hollow boast, for at one point he does describe inquiries which he had made personally concerning the country around Daras.[15] As we read this brief passage, we can catch a flash of the old Procopius of the *History of the Wars*: innately curious and anxious to explore. He must have had a fund of recollections like these on which he could draw if he wished. Yet, so little of Procopius' personality intrudes into the *Buildings* that it is hard to believe he wrote it happily.

II   *The Treatment of Justinian*

In the *Buildings,* all construction work in the empire, no matter how small the project, was Justinian's doing. As Procopius portrayed him, it was he who pulled down an old fortress in Cappadocia, devised a plan to save Tarsus from floods, and solved engineering problems which baffled the architects of Hagia Sophia, to cite only three examples out of many.[16] By dint of much looking, scholars have found some traces of concealed hostility to the emperor, such as a possible, though obscure reference to the *Secret History*,[17] a rather strange comparison with Sirius, the Dog Star, which in classical literature brought destruction, when Procopius is describing the equestrian statue of Justinian in Constantinople,[18] and the occasional double entendre which seems to indicate that Justinian's generosity was really closer to extravagance.[19] Yet, all these hints amount to very little. In general, Procopius' compliments are cool, but they are correct, and his praise is abundant.

The Justinian of the *Buildings* is the conventional Byzantine emperor, the vicegerent of God, and the friend of the *Logos* or Divine Word (Christ was the *logos* made flesh while He was on earth, according to the opening words of the Gospel of Saint John), and the shepherd of his people. Byzantine literature has much to say on what the virtues and duties of a true *basileus* are, and from Justinian to the end of the empire, the ideal picture changes very little. He should succor his subjects in famine and earthquake, build public works, endow schools and universities, and protect the poor against the rich and powerful. He was not divine, nor, for all his trappings, was he an Oriental despot; yet the conceptual framework of his position was inherited from the divine kings of the Hellenistic world, and Hellenistic doctrines of kingship reappear in Byzantium.

We can recognize them under Constantine, the first Christian emperor. Eusebius of Caesarea, who was also the founder of Christian history, laid down the outlines of Christian *basileia* in an oration composed in honor of the thirtieth anniversary of Constantine's reign: "He it is—the Word of God proceeding above all things and through all things, and in all things, both visible and invisible—who is Lord of all the Universe; from whom and through whom the king (*basileus*), the beloved of God, receives and bears the image of His Supreme Kingship, and so steers and directs, in imitation of his Superior, the helm of all the affairs of this world."[20] There was no place for divine kings in the Christian empire, but in Eusebius' hands, the concept of divine kingship was adapted to fit the new order. The emperor was no longer a god himself; instead, he became the representative of God on earth, and his empire was a reflection of the Heavenly Kingdom.[21] With Justinian, this fusion of Hellenistic and Christian ideas even received legal sanction. In one of Justinian's novels,[22] for the first time in Roman law, the emperor is named *nomos empsychos* or "incarnate law," as were the Hellenistic kings.

Thus, the Roman emperor became the Byzantine sacerdotal *basileus*. We should make qualifications immediately: the emperor was the vicegerent of God, but he was not a priest; he could not administer the sacraments, although he could, if he wished, deliver a sermon in church. He was never infallible in matters of Christian dogma.[23] The kings of the Hellenistic world may have been divine, but they were never omnipotent. (Pagan gods, as anyone who has read Homer knows, shared all the human vices.) Perhaps Constantine had a better power base as the vicegerent of one all-powerful God than any divine king in the pagan world, who had to compete with a vast number of major and minor divinities who claimed attention. However, both the divine kings and the sacerdotal *basileus* laid stress in their propaganda on services to their subjects. Justinian, as portrayed in the *Buildings,* is not only a divinely inspired vice-gerent of God; he is also a "service monarch" laboring for his people. Procopius loses no opportunity to display the emperor's divine inspiration. He describes at length the magnificence of the great church of Hagia Sophia, but he continues, "Not by money alone did the emperor build it, but with the labor of his intellect, and especially the virtue of his soul, as I shall demonstrate forthwith."[24] Twice during the erection of the church,[25] it was in danger of collapse, and the architects Anthemius and Isidorus, who were themselves at a loss what to do, turned to Justinian for help. He, "inspired," writes Procopius, "I do not know from where, but I think from God," and solved their problems. Procopius claims that many witnesses would corroborate his story and concludes, "In this way, the emperor is provided with a testimonial from the work."[26]

On the Persian frontier, God cooperated with Justinian in a remarkable fashion in order to make the fortress of Daras impregnable. The river which brought water into the city flowed through a gorge, so that no enemy could tamper with it and take Daras by cutting off its water supply. But when it left Daras, it wound through the adjoining plain, and provided a good supply of water for any enemy who wanted to pitch camp there. Here was an impossible problem. But, writes Procopius, God provided the solution. He showed the Romans an alternative underground channel for the river as it left the city, and afterward, the defenders of Daras could divert the river at will, either to water the plain or to deny water to an enemy encamped there.[27] A little later in the text, Procopius provides further proof of the emperor's supernatural intelligence. An engineer in Alexandria saw in a dream a device to prevent flooding in Daras. He sent a letter describing this device to the emperor, but as it happened, the emperor himself had already suggested exactly the same device to his engineers. Thus, it was clear that Justinian tapped a source of superhuman wisdom.[28]

Whenever Procopius gets the chance, he points out how the emperor also fulfilled his function of extending Christianity. For the Tzani, he built a church at a place called Schamalinichon and made them worship God "so that they should be aware that they are human beings." The Samaritans for the most part were converted by the emperor. At Awjila in Libya, where a pagan cult was still flourishing, Justinian brought it to an end, and erected a church to the Mother of God. Even the sparsely populated regions of the empire felt Justinian's care and service. Cyrenaica in North Africa was mostly desert, Procopius noted, but still Justinian took thought to secure it from inroads of the Moors. God was always the emperor's partner, and He lent him advice and support, even when everyone else held back.[29]

One could go on. It is not surprising to find Justinian portrayed in the conventional manner as the sacerdotal emperor. Panegyrics generally deal with conventional concepts. What is surprising is to discover the same concept turned upside down in the *Secret History*. There Justinian also has supernatural help, but it is to create destruction rather than to care for his subjects and to serve God. He is everything an ideal *basileus* should not be: not the vicegerent of God, but the prince of the devils.

CHAPTER 4

The Secret History

I *The Problem*

THE *Secret History* remains a mystery, and for this reason, and also because the public has a nose for pornography, it has attracted more popular attention than Procopius' other works. We do not know what title Procopius gave it, if any. As I have already pointed out, the *Souda,* which is the first source to mention it by name, titles it the "so-called Anekdota," or "unpublished writings," and treats it as if it were a final, ninth book of the *Wars*—a view to which the preface lends some force, for it states that the purpose of the work is to provide information which had to be suppressed in the published history. Yet Procopius imagines himself addressing an audience of readers, so that presumably he looked forward to eventual publication. His audience is one educated like himself, equipped to appreciate the borrowing of a phrase here and an expression there from the classical authors. It is presumably an audience which is living after Justinian is dead, for Procopius refers to Justinian and Theodora in the past tense. But the *Secret History* concludes with a sentence which makes it clear that the emperor was still alive when Procopius reached the end of his libelous little essay.

The first problem is presented by the opening words. They are strangely similar to those which began the eighth book of the *Wars*; although they do not repeat each other exactly, they have the same meaning. But though the preface fits the eighth book very well, it is out of place at the beginning of the *Secret History.*[1] As in the eighth book, Procopius states that he is going to set down in the *Secret History* everything which occurred everywhere in the Roman Empire: that is, he will no longer deal with the wars in Asia, Libya, and Italy, in three separate sections, as he had done in the *History of the*

Wars. In the eighth book, that was precisely what he had intended to do. However, in the *Secret History,* his intention was not to set down everything which happened, but simply the information which he had had to suppress in the published version of the *Wars.* He went on with a curious statement, since he was writing while Justinian still lived:

. . . For here I shall write down everything which chanced to take place everywhere in the Roman Empire. The reason for this is that, while the perpetrators of the deeds were still alive, I could not describe them as they ought to have been. For neither could I elude the watchfulness of vast numbers of spies, nor escape a most cruel death, if I were found out.[2]

The reference to imperial spies may deserve more than passing notice. (Later, Procopius is to claim that Justinian allowed the intelligence service to decay.)[3] Had Procopius experienced their efficiency? Can we have here a covert reference to what we have already suspected, that the eighth book of the *Wars* gave some offense when it was published and that conceivably some government official denounced Procopius? Was the *Buildings* Procopius' penance and the *Secret History* his revenge?

Arguments about the *Secret History* tend to be overly subtle, and I have no wish to add to them. The remainder of this preface is full of conventional sentiments borrowed from historiographical tradition. Procopius even claims a moral purpose for writing: evil in the future will reflect on the punishment which befell the scoundrels he describes, and they will be deterred by fear that their misdeeds too, if they commit any, will be put on record by some future Procopius. How these sentiments apply to the *Secret History* is not easy to say. Procopius tells of no punishment which befell Justinian and Theodora. (Belisarius' cross seems to have been marriage to Antonina.) Whether future tyrants would be deterred by secret historians is an open question. However, apart from conventional sentiments, the message of the preface is that the *Secret History* would provide information which had to be omitted from the *History of the Wars* because it was too dangerous to publish. For the first section of the work, which deals with Belisarius and his wife, in length about one-sixth of the total, the *Secret History* is little more than a commentary on the earlier work. Then Procopius switches his attention to Justinian and Theodora and gives himself freer rein, although he does not entirely forget his original purpose.

II   *The Veracity of the* Secret History

The veracity of the *Secret History* is another, more vexing problem. There is a paranoid style to it which should make the reader wary of putting too much trust in it. But bias and exaggeration of facts is one thing; outright falsehood is another. We can corroborate some of the information which the *Secret History* gives, and it is true, as Bury said, that "in no instance can we convict him [Procopius] of a statement which has no basis in fact."[4] However, Bury was following the principle that an historian should be considered innocent of prevarication until proved guilty, for much of the lurid detail in the *Secret History* is found nowhere else. For instance, it is our only source for Empress Theodora's early life and for the details of some of the palace intrigues attributed to her. Was she really the daughter of a bearkeeper in the circus? Was she an actress in the theater and a prostitute with an alarming sexual appetite before she married Justinian? Did she really instigate the Gothic king Theodatus to put Amalasuntha to death? We owe our knowledge of all these tidbits to the *Secret History.*

The reputation of Theodora in the Byzantine world was very different. From at least the ninth century, tradition praised her as wise, pure in soul, and lovely in body. She was compared with Saint Helena, mother of Constantine the Great. As we might expect, the Monophysite church celebrated her memory, for she was its ally. A Syriac legend, which was current in the twelfth century, said that her father was a pious old man, strongly Monophysite. When Justinian asked for her hand in marriage, the father made him swear that he would never force Theodora to accept the accursed doctrine of Chalcedon. Even Procopius, giving the official opinion of her beauty in his *Buildings,* written after her death, says that her loveliness was beyond words.[5] We may suspect that Procopius has overdrawn his picture of the empress to titillate his readers, and it is worth recalling that the *Souda,* as well as giving us the first notice of the *Secret History,* remarks that it contains "censure and comedy directed against the emperor Justinian and his wife Theodora, as well as Belisarius himself, and his wife." Procopius, as the *Souda* realized, intended his readers to be amused as well as impressed by his revelations. Yet, with due allowance for its viewpoint, the censure in the *Secret History* deserves to be taken seriously.

We can find some corroboration in a Syriac source for Procopius' story of Theodora's past before she married Justinian. John of Ephesus was a Monophysite bishop, a friend and protégé of Theodora. As well as being a phenomenally successful missionary, he was the most important early historian writing in Syriac. We would expect him to deal fairly with the reputation of the empress, who had defended the Monophysite cause. Yet, at one point, he calls her rather brutally, "Theodora *ek tou porneiou*," or "Theodora from the brothel," though without appearing to reproach her in any way by this epithet, which seems to have been taken over in a matter-of-fact manner from the Greek. But it is enough to demonstrate that Procopius' story was not a fabrication. The story that Theodora was a prostitute before her marriage was built around a solid kernel of truth, even though there may be some embroidery.[6]

We should remember that Byzantium accepted commoners as empresses much more readily than the Victorians, and Theodora was not the only woman of lowly origin to reach the throne. What mattered was not that she had been a whore, but that she had repented, and even Procopius can cite no evidence of loose living against her after she married Justinian.[7] Presumably she had already reformed by the time Justinian met her, for Byzantine tradition had it that she was living then in a humble house, where she spent her time spinning wool like an ancient Roman matron. On the site of this house she erected the church of Saint Panteleimon once she became empress. Procopius tells us that she attacked prostitution in Constantinople with what he clearly regarded as unnatural zeal.[8] She took some five hundred cheap whores, who plied their trade in the marketplace, selling themselves to all takers for a few cents, and dispatched them to the Convent of Repentance, which she had established for such ladies. There the life of virtue which these prostitutes were compelled to adopt drove some of them to suicide.

That Theodora was an actress is likely enough; it finds some indirect corroboration in Justinian's law code. The *Secret History* states that, in order to marry Theodora, Justinian had to persuade his uncle Justin to change the law forbidding senators to marry courtesans,[9] and the code records the necessary change. The fate of the Gothic queen Amalasuntha is another problem. The secret historian has it that Theodora gave Justinian's envoy, Peter, private instructions to arrange for Amalasuntha's death. Yet, according to the account given by Procopius in his *Gothic War,* Theodatus had Amalasuntha murdered at the instigation of her enemies among the Goths, and when Peter reached Italy, she was already dead.[10] Both stories cannot be true, although this is the only instance I can cite where the author of the *Wars* and the author of the *Secret History* flatly contradict each other. Most modern historians assume that the version in the *Secret History* is without any basis in fact.

On the other hand, it may not be a complete fabrication. Theodora was carrying on some mysterious negotiation with the Ostrogothic court about the time of Amalasuntha's murder. As evidence of this we can cite a letter to Theodora from Theodatus' queen, Gudelina, which refers to an unspecified request the empress had made.[11] Apparently it had been carried out. In context, the request can hardly have been for the death of Amalasuntha. Yet, in the secretive world of Byzantine diplomacy, it was easy for rumors to arise, and Procopius was glad to believe any tale which illustrated Theodora's villainy. He told the truth as he saw it, even though he selected details with a malevolent eye.

One other story, to which Procopius only alludes, illustrates the seamy side of palace intrigue with which the *Secret History* deals. Early in his essay,[12] Procopius promises to tell how Belisarius and Antonina deposed Pope Silverius. He never fulfills this promise, although later he indicates that Antonina used a man named Eugenius in this connection to perform an unholy act, presumably the murder of the Pope.[13] In the *Gothic War,* Procopius had mentioned that Silverius had urged the Romans to receive Belisarius' army peaceably into their city in 536. But shortly thereafter, during the siege of Rome, Belisarius dismissed Silverius on suspicion of treason and replaced him with Vigilius.[14] Nothing more. When juxtaposed, these two morsels of information sound strangely contradictory: in the first, Silverius was a friend and partisan; in the second he was suspected of helping the Goths; but Procopius makes no comment.

However, the biography of Silverius in the *Liber Pontificalis* adds some interesting details. Theodora was convinced that Silverius, a stubborn adherent of the doctrines of Chalcedon, had to be replaced by Vigilius, who promised to be more flexible. Belisarius and Antonina acted as her agents. The pope was summoned to the Pincian palace where Belisarius had his headquarters. On entering, he was conducted to an inner room, while the clergy who attended him were told to wait outside. In the room was Antonina sitting on her bed, with Belisarius at her feet. As the pope entered, Antonina broke out, "Tell us, sir pope Silverius, what have we done to you and the Romans that you want to betray us into the hands of the Goths?" Thereupon, a subdeacon entered, tore the pallium from the pope's shoulders, took him to another room, and dressed him in a monk's habit. He was then displayed to the waiting clergy, who were informed that the pope was deposed and had become a monk. Presumably, it was a story of this sort which Procopius intended to include in his *Secret History,* but for some reason he omitted it. Exactly what the role of the servant Eugenius may have been is not clear.

The story of Silverius serves to demonstrate that the world of intrigue portrayed in the *Secret History* is not fantasy. If Theodora and Antonina could act together with Belisarius' connivance to rid the empire of Silverius, we need not disbelieve the other misdeeds which Procopius attributes to that alliance. Though Procopius may interpret the facts malevolently, he does not lose sight of them. He repeats hearsay and rumor, but we cannot convict him of outright falsehood. What puts the *Secret History* apart from the *Wars* is a matter of viewpoint. The *Wars* had contained criticism, but usually veiled in phraseology borrowed from the classics, and affecting an Olympian detachment. The *Secret History* was written with undisguised hatred, though, for Belisarius, the feeling is perhaps less hatred than disgust. However, for Antonina, his ill will is intense, and for Justinian and Theodora, it is apocalyptic.

Modern historians have tried to produce various explanations. One has suggested that Procopius was a secret heretic himself and presumably resented Justinian because of his attempt to enforce orthodoxy.[15] But the evidence for this must be supplied by our imagination. Procopius' attitude toward the theological disputes of his own day seems to have been pragmatic and slightly skeptical.[16] One scholar has compared him to a Herbert Spencer[17] trying to comprehend a nineteenth-century German idealist philosopher. Heresy does not provide the answer.

Perhaps Procopius' later career would provide part of the explanation, if we knew more about it. As we have already seen, Belisarius was temporarily in disgrace, and under suspicion of treason in 543; according to the *Secret History*,[18] many of his friends were forbidden to visit him. By this point, Procopius may have ceased to be Belisarius' secretary, but this veto must have affected him nevertheless. Conceivably, it may have interrupted his own career in the imperial bureaucracy. Forced to resume his old profession as a *rhetor* or professional pleader in the courts, he discovered that Justinian's judicial reforms had made *rhetores* more or less superfluous. He complains that Belisarius failed to honor pledges made to certain of his friends, and perhaps among these broken pledges were some made to Procopius. We do not know. The *Secret History* tells us much about Procopius' psychology, but nowhere does it give us any extra biographical information.

There is one hint which may help to explain why Procopius felt the way he did about his former hero, Belisarius. Belisarius' fault was that he was weak and uxorious, completely dominated by his wife, Antonina. At one point, he speculates that she had bewitched him,[19] for he could not account for her ascendancy over him in any other way. In fact, he does provide us with a reason for the domination, even though he refused to recognize it himself. Antonina was Theodora's crony and thus had better access to power and influence at court than did Belisarius himself. However, Procopius clearly disliked dominating women with questionable morals, and he could not condone the way Belisarius allowed his wife to behave.

It appears from the *Secret History* that Belisarius reached a turning point in Procopius' regard about 544, when he was reappointed to the command of the war against the Ostrogoths. By then, he had suffered disgrace and indignity himself, and he knew the truth about his wife's infidelities. Everyone believed (according to Procopius) that he wanted the command in Italy so that he could rebel at the first opportunity[20] and punish those who had wronged him, and his wife into the bargain. But Belisarius disappointed "everyone," an anonymous group which no doubt included Procopius and his friends. He remained loyal.

It is only a hint, but we are probably right in thinking that at about this time, some enemies of the regime were hoping that Belisarius would rid the world of Justinian. Afterward, he was a light that failed.

III   *The Criticisms*

The criticisms voiced by Procopius in the *Secret History* fall generally into three categories. First, there are those which make good omissions in the *History of the Wars* and divulge causes for events which had had to be concealed in the earlier work. The majority of this group can be found in the first section, which deals with Belisarius and Antonina, but we should also include in this category a number which amplify passing animadversions in the *Wars*. All of these fulfill in some measure the purpose which Procopius stated in his preface to the *Secret History*; they set down what he had not dared to write in his published work.

Then there is a group of self-interested criticisms, which make up the majority. These are bitter, but still completely rational, and explicable in political and sociological terms. They reflect the views of the traditional elite of the empire, the educated, landowning class with which Procopius identified himself, which was conservative in its outlook and hated innovations. Finally, there is a category which is apocalyptic and which attempted to explain the age of Justinian in chiliastic terms. We should of course, be in no hurry to call this type irrational, for Procopius belonged to a society which thought in theological terms, much as our own thinks in scientific ones. These three varieties of criticisms are worth separate examination.

First, those which make good omissions and amplify criticisms latent in the *Wars*. A few instances will illustrate. I have already referred to the instance in the *Gothic War* where Belisarius quarreled with one of his officers, Constantinus, over a pair of daggers which Constantinus had stolen from a civilian. The quarrel ended with Belisarius ordering Constantinus executed. This was an unholy deed, remarked Procopius, but one not characteristic of Belisarius. In the *Secret History,* Procopius amplifies the background of this brief story. Belisarius had learned that his wife had a lover and ordered his servants to put him to death; however, the lover escaped. Constantinus saw that Belisarius was downcast, and, by way of indicating his sympathy, told him that if he had been the man cuckolded, he would have killed the wife rather than the lover.[21]

Procopius claims that Antonina found out about this remark and awaited an opportunity for revenge. When the affair of the daggers occurred, Belisarius was willing to let Constantinus go free, but Antonina insisted that he die. The "unholy deed" was Antonina's doing.

The friction between Belisarius and another of his officers in Italy, John, nephew of Vitalian, was well documented in the *Wars*. Reason for the friction appeared to be that John, an independent but able general, held Ariminum against Belisarius' orders. Consequently, he was besieged there by the Goths. Belisarius, for good strategic reasons which John failed to appreciate, very nearly allowed him to starve before relieving him. The *Secret History* claims that Theodora persecuted John because he had married a daughter of Germanus, whom she disliked. John, who knew that Antonina was the Empress' creature and Belisarius was Antonina's, was afraid to meet Belisarius for fear that he might be murdered.[22]

There are other instances. In 545, a Byzantine officer named Herodian went over to the Goths and surrendered Spoletium to them. The *Wars* had claimed that he defected because Belisarius had threatened to look into his past record, which, presumably, did not bear examination. The *Secret History* states that the real reason for Herodian's disaffection was that Belisarius hounded him for money.[23] Procopius had excoriated the incompetence of Sergius, the nephew of Solomon, who was appointed governor of Libya after Solomon lost his life fighting the Moors. The *Secret History*[24] adds that Sergius was a suitor for Antonina's daughter, and Theodora protected him to do Antonina a favor, although she was well aware that he was unfit for his position. In the *Wars,* the business of making history was 95 percent a male task. In the *Secret History,* Procopius swung to the other extreme, seeing the malevolent influence of these two lewd, improper females, Theodora and Antonina, everywhere.

Criticisms of Justinian, at which the *Wars* had only hinted, are elaborated in the *Secret History*. An abortive conspiracy against Justinian, led by two disaffected Armenians, took place in 548. In a speech which Procopius assigns to one of the traitors, he characterizes Justinian as a man who sat unguarded in some lobby to late hours, unrolling the Scripture with aged priests, and arguing theology.[25] The *Secret History* declares that Justinian and Theodora were the cause of strife among the Christians.[26] Procopius suggested in the *Wars* that Justinian forgave his commanders' errors too readily, and as a result, most of them were guilty of offenses in private life, or against the state.[27] The *Secret History* says flatly that Justinian's easygoing nature caused instability.[28] Envoys dispatched to Persia by Wittigis are made to say in the *Wars* that Justinian was an innovator who loved things which did not belong to him, and could not allow established customs to remain intact.[29] The *Secret History* expatiates on this theme again and again.[30]

The *Wars* had questioned imperial policies toward the barbarians, although it did so with circumspection.[31] For instance, Procopius reported what he claimed was popular opinion, that the armistice Justinian made with Persia in 542 surrendered Lazica.[32] But, having reproduced this criticism, he immediately added that he could not say whether or not it was justified. He assumed the mask of Herodotus, who had said that a historian must report what he heard, though he need not believe it. Who could be so insensible to literature as to blame Procopius for following Herodotus' example?

There was no need to be circumspect in the *Secret History,* and Procopius treated the policy of Justinian toward the barbarians as so much madness. He accused him of stirring up trouble[33] and of wasting the empire's resources on huge donatives.[34] In the anterooms of the palace, poor fellows who were waiting to transact business would quarrel over where the money of the Romans had gone: some said that the emperor kept it all locked away, others, that the barbarians had every cent of it.[35] The impression which the *Secret History* conveys is that Justinian wasted enormous subsidies on the barbarians, not merely to buy them off, but in a deliberate effort to empty the treasury.

Yet, in point of fact, this criticism was less than just. Emperors long before Justinian had used subsidies as part of their defense arsenal, and it was not an unwise policy. Campaigns with professional armies were extremely expensive, and Roman governments often found it more economical to buy off the barbarians than to fight them. Moreover, a recent estimate of what Justinian spent on subsidies puts it at no more than 2 percent of the total annual revenue, and this was about the same proportion as the emperor

Anastasius spent for the same purpose, although Procopius singled out Anastasius for praise. In fact, we know that the Persians received a higher annual subsidy under Anastasius than they did under Justinian.[36]

Second, there are the self-interested criticisms which reflect the views of the traditional elite of the empire. Procopius claimed that Justinian plundered the wealthy[37] and cites an instance where he mulcted an heiress (a lady who lived in Caesarea) of three-quarters of her father's estate by changing the law of inheritance.[38] He degraded the senatorial order and stripped it of its property.[39] One result of this was that the legal profession had nothing left to do, for their senatorial clients were impoverished and could not carry on any litigation because they had nothing left to litigate about.[40] Another facet of Justinian's behavior which aroused the historian's indignation was his way of making himself accessible to everyone, including the lower classes[41]—a criticism which may strike us as strange, until we remember that the emperor's approachability made it easier for cases to be brought directly before him, reducing the perquisites of the go-betweens. He exacted taxes and requisitions harshly. "This emperor from the first was more ruthless than all the barbarians put together,"[42] Procopius stated extravagantly, and the money he collected was wasted senselessly. We may note that among the emperor's wasteful projects advertised in the *Secret History* was his extravagant building.[43]

These are all complaints which we would associate with a right-wing conservative who had special interests to protect. Procopius was himself a senator; imperial measures which touched the senatorial order affected him personally. Legal reforms which diminished the perquisites of his profession as *rhetor* must have lowered his own income.[44] The complaints that taxes were too high and that the government was wasting money are not surprising; they are common enough today, but they are particularly prevalent among the propertied class which has something to lose to the revenue collectors.

Some of the criticisms reveal a lively disdain for upstarts with the wrong background and the wrong school ties. As successor to Tribonian, who chaired the commission which drew up the new code of law (Procopius notes his avarice),[45] Justinian appointed a Libyan, Junilus (otherwise unknown), whose Greek was abominable, [46] who was not even a *rhetor* and who knew nothing about the law. Junilus' successor was not much better; he knew something about law, but he was too young. The empress Theodora, for whom Justinian developed an inordinate sexual passion, was below his station. As emperor, he could have chosen any wellborn woman he wanted as wife[47]—a fact which made his marriage to the much-vilified Theodora all the more unnatural. As for Theodora herself, one of her sins was that she had no regard for the class structure of the empire. Procopius describes how she charged two sisters, who were sprung from three generations of consuls, of having affairs with low-born lovers, and forced them to marry these men, much against the better judgment of the two ladies involved.[48] Justinian himself acted like a barbarian, and his Greek was accented. We should remember that the emperor was of Illyrian peasant stock, and his native tongue was Latin, not Greek. He was not, as Procopius was, a product of one of the best schools of the Hellenized East, and this was an age when education was the chief determinant of social status.

The *Secret History* also betrays a curious fascination with sex. In her heyday as a courtesan, Theodora exhausted ten lusty young men and then did the same for their thirty attendants. Her famous act in the theater had been to strip off as many of her clothes as the law allowed (burlesque queens were not permitted to remove their girdles); then to sprawl back on the ground and allow slaves to sprinkle barley on her private parts, which a gaggle of geese proceeded to pick up with their beaks. After the performance was over, Procopius reports that she had not even the grace to blush.[49]

Both Justinian and Belisarius are represented as prisoners of sexual passion for their wives. This thralldom to Antonina ruined Belisarius, who was weak, yet not innately bad; but Justinian and Theodora were well-matched partners in wickedness. Strangest of all Procopius' complaints is his claim that all women in Byzantium became corrupt and faithless. When their husbands tried to discipline them, they appealed to the empress, and she protected them from condign punishment.[50]

These are only a selection of the self-interested criticisms making up the bulk of Procopius' invective. They betray the viewpoint of a traditionalist, suspicious of change. He was also a man with a vested interest. As a *rhetor,* his professional standing was affected by Justinian's legal innovations; as a senator, his social standing was imperiled. Procopius' outlook was narrow, and perhaps bigoted, but no more than we should expect. Highly trained professionals are rarely pleased to find that their skills are obsolete, and there are few people nowadays who will not fight to maintain their social standing.

This is not to say that Procopius was entirely unfair. Taxation was crushing, and it was exacted according to the principle of collective responsibility, which encouraged injustices. When Procopius complained that, at the time the plague was sweeping the empire, the emperor made proprietors of estates responsible for the taxes of their deceased neighbors, he was describing what must have been regular procedure.[51] But note that Procopius spoke *ex parte*; the victims he cited were senators or large landowners, not peasants whose sufferings were even greater. We have here echoes of the long and somewhat obscure struggle which Justinian carried on with the large proprietors of the empire—a struggle which survived him, and which the emperors eventually lost.

Could Procopius have suffered from any confiscations himself? He does tell an intriguing story of how a *rhetor* from his own native city of Caesarea had made a little money and used it to purchase a village on the seashore, whereupon Justinian expropriated the village, giving the *rhetor* only a fraction of its value.[52] One suspects that Procopius learned of this transaction from the victim himself, and we may even wonder if he was not Procopius. But the *Secret History* gives no hint of the *rhetor's* identity, and we should hesitate to make hasty conclusions. Nor need we attribute his misogynist streak to personal experience. He was a product of what modern communications experts call a traditional "male vanity culture,"[53] which imputes wisdom to its male elders and believes firmly that women should play a passive role. His ideal woman was the opposite of Antonina and Theodora.

The criticisms which I have labeled "apocalyptic" are of a different sort. They seem to spring from the realization that not all the disasters of the reign could be attributed to human causes; plague, floods, and earthquakes were beyond the power of ordinary mortals. Running through the *Secret History* is the suggestion that Justinian had superhuman assistance in bringing destruction on the empire, and eventually the suggestion becomes explicit. Procopius indicates that he and many of his friends felt that Justinian was the opposite of the true *basileus*; he was not the vicegerent of God but the prince of devils, whom we can identify in theological terms as the Antichrist.[54]

To give his theory some verisimilitude, Procopius quoted a number of stories which must have been borrowed from the gossip circulating in his own social stratum. The first comes from the early career of Justin. While he was still an ordinary soldier, his commander jailed him and intended to execute him, but a vision of a creature larger than human size appeared three times and ordered Justin's release. For, the apparition said, some time in the future, when he wanted an instrument of his wrath, he might have use for Justin and his family.[55]

Justinian's mother was supposed to have said that, on the night she conceived him, she was visited by an invisible demon.[56] Some men who worked late into the night with Justinian claimed that they had seen his head leave his body and then return.[57] Perhaps the most dramatic evidence came from a monk who had arrived at the palace to present a petition on behalf of his monastery. When he was admitted to the emperor's presence, he recoiled and acted like a man struck dumb. Later, when his attendants asked him what had happened, he told them that he had seen the prince of devils seated on the throne.[58]

Justinian ate little, worked day and night, and never seemed in need of sleep.[59] In physical appearance, he resembled the emperor Domitian, who was one of the traditional archetypes of the Antichrist.[60] All these were characteristics which contributed to the general impression of satanic power.

There were also stories about Theodora. Before she became Justinian's wife, it was said that she had had a dream which foretold that she would marry the prince of demons.[61] Another tale related how some men who had been Theodora's lovers while she was still in the theater claimed that sometimes a spirit of some sort came into her bedroom at night and drove them out.[62] We may wonder if Procopius really remained faithful to his principle of personal observation when he collected this particular story. Had he interviewed Theodora's former lovers? Or was he simply repeating gossip?

In one telling passage, Procopius said that he, like most of his contemporaries, felt that Justinian and Theodora were demons because their power to wreak destruction surpassed anything that a human, however terrible, had possessed in the past,[63] because *tyche* cooperated with them in their aims. *Tyche,* which we translate not altogether adequately by "chance" or "fortune," was an inheritance from the classical past, and the role which it plays in Procopius' history is a subject we must postpone for later discussion. At this point, it is enough to say that chance in Procopius is never completely blind; behind it, there is always divine power. Yet *tyche* had sent plagues and earthquakes to help Justinian destroy the empire, and, in theological terms, the explanation had to be that the emperor's power came from the devil. Procopius writes: "I shall demonstrate how many evils he did mankind with his concealed power and demonic nature. For while this monarch was administering the affairs of state, as it chanced, much other suffering took place, which some men insisted was brought about because this evil demon was among us, and contrived to produce it, and others that the Power of the Divine, loathing his works, turned away from the Roman empire, and allowed abominable devils to bring about these mis-fortunes. . . ."[64]

The Justinian of the *Secret History* is the complete opposite of the sacerdotal emperor as portrayed in the *Buildings*. In the *Buildings,* Justinian was divinely inspired; he was God's representative on earth and had the cooperation of God in fulfilling his imperial func-tion.[65] In the *Secret History,* he is also the bearer of supernatural power, but it is an infernal power which he used for destruction. He is not the vicegerent of God but the prince of demons, and the powers of evil cooperated with him to bring destruction. Since it is likely that the *Secret History* and the *Buildings* were written at the same time, together they give us a graphic picture of the public and private Procopius, in direct opposition to each other.

We may conclude that Procopius' hatred of Justinian was basically that of a member of the traditional elite for an innovator whose re-forms reduced the wealth and power of his own group. But this was the Byzantine world, impregnated with theology, and looking to the Kingdom of Heaven as its model. It required no great intellectual leap for Procopius to hold Justinian responsible for the natural dis-asters of his reign. If he could be responsible for the engineering wizardry which made the building of Hagia Sophia possible, as the public Procopius proclaimed, why not an earthquake?

Yet this logic led to one inexorable conclusion. Something was wrong with the order of things in the empire if *tyche* could cooperate with the emperor to bring disasters. Procopius turned the concept of the sacerdotal *basileus* on its head. Justinian was not the vicegerent of God. He was the Antichrist.

CHAPTER 5

The Intellectual Odyssey
of Procopius

THE double vision of Procopius, which I have analyzed in the previous chapter, is apparent to anyone who dips into his works. Far from being a mystery, the antithesis of the public Procopius and the secret historian has a certain logic to it, if we examine it against the background of the late Roman thought world. The next question which arises is by what stages Procopius reached his conclusion that Justinian was the Antichrist and that Belisarius was a weak man condemned by God for his sins. I have already indicated my belief that this was a conviction which grew on Procopius during the course of his career. It remains to examine the internal evidence in Procopius' works in order to mark out the clues, if any, which tell how Procopius' bitter outlook grew upon him.

I   The Outlook of Procopius in the History of the Wars

In the spring of A.D. 533, Belisarius and his wife Antonina sailed from Constantinople against the Vandal kingdom in Africa. With them in the flagship was Procopius, who, he tells us, "earlier had been frightened at the danger, but later he saw a vision in a dream which encouraged him, and made him eager for the expedition."[1] In his dream, he saw Belisarius and his men lying on the soil of Africa and eating its fruits. And so Procopius, with mixed fear and anticipation, set off with the fleet.

His optimism was always tempered by caution and literary training. As he feasted in Gelimer's palace in Carthage later in the same year, he reflected how the power of fortune (*tyche*) had given victory to the imperial forces. *Tyche* was an ancient goddess borrowed from the traditions of classical historiography, and Procopius pauses occasionally in his *History* to reflect on her importance. Yet though his optimism is guarded, it is present. The Procopius who sailed for Africa in 533 was a different man from the embittered senator who wrote the *Secret History* to correct the impression which his *Wars* had conveyed.

His education had already molded his outlook. As we have seen, he knew Latin, but his acquaintance with Latin literature was slight. Probably he had read the *Aeneid* at school, or parts of it, for Latin students in sixth-century Palestine seem to have cut their teeth on Virgil much as their modern counterparts do on Julius Caesar. He knew the story of how Dido founded Carthage,[2] and he devoted a long passage to the ship of Aeneas,[3] which he saw at the Navalia in Rome. In Rome too, he knew the house of the historian Sallust,[4] but he does not indicate how far his acquaintance with Sallust's writings extended. He seems to have become acquainted with some senatorial families; at least he can give his readers some details of the sufferings they endured during the Gothic War.

But to judge from what he considered most worthy of comment on his travels, he was more at home with the mythological period than he was with the eight hundred years or so of history which ended in 476. For instance, he says that before the Moors immigrated into Libya, the area was inhabited by autochthonous people,[5] and as proof, he cites the legend of how Heracles wrestled with a king of Libya, Antaeus, who was the son of the earth.[6] Italy provided many reminders of the mythological past. As the Byzantine army marched through the *mezzogiorno,* it reached the town of Beneventum, which Procopius singled out for mention. The Romans had won a famous victory there over Pyrrhus, king of Epirus, in 275 B.C. However, Procopius omits all mention of it. Instead, he relates the story of how Beneventum was founded by Diomedes, son of Tydeus, whose exploits were told in the *Iliad.*[7]

In contrast to the immediacy of the mythological past, the history of the Roman Empire before the end of the fourth century seems lost in the mists of time. As Procopius was describing the famous siege of Rome by Wittigis in 536–37, he noted how "the Romans of old" had built a double wall called the Vivarium at one point in the circumvallation. They did this, not to strengthen the wall, but to make an enclosed space called a "vivarium" where they could keep lions and other wild animals for the wild beast fights staged in the amphitheaters, a "kind of luxury which was improper."[8] Procopius seems separated from these "Romans of old" by a great gulf of time and manners, although we should remember that neither gladiatorial games nor wild-beast fights won the following in the eastern provinces of the Roman Empire that they did in the West. Procopius' barely disguised contempt may have been partly the disdain of an educated Greek for a non-Greek custom.[9]

This is not simply a case of Procopius assuming his customary classical mask. His outlook in the *Buildings,* where he wore the mask less securely, was the same. He spoke there of the "ancient emperor, Septimius Severus,"[10] who ruled from 193 to 211, but he mentioned the battle of the Lapiths and the centaurs with easy familiarity.[11] When he described Thermopylae in Greece, he assumed without question that his readers had heard about the famous battle there, when Leonidas and his three hundred Spartiates died defending the pass against the Persians.[12] The unfamiliar "ancient world" of Procopius seems to have been the seven centuries which followed Alexander the Great.

Perhaps this is what we should expect. The Byzantine schools in the sixth century neglected this period to concentrate on the classical authors. As we have seen, Procopius took as models Herodotus and Thucydides, both belonging to the approved period. Yet this education could produce a certain ambivalence toward his own day. To give an instance: we have already remarked on the evidence for Procopius' conservatism and his distrust of innovation, which was the hallmark of evil monarchs like Justinian and Chosroes. Yet, Herodotus had no such distrust, and Thucydides actually believed in progress.[13] To wear his classical mask correctly, Procopius had to pay his formal respects to progress too, and he did. In his introduction to the *History of the Wars,* he devoted a brief section to progress in military science, citing as an example improvements in archery.[14] Again in his eighth book, he attacked those men who believed that everything ancient was sound and honorable, and despised what was contemporary.[15] Procopius did not consider himself a reactionary, and in certain aspects, he was not.

In particular, his outlook on the science of warfare was up to date and professional. He noted how the Vandals lacked archers and javelin-throwers (their men fought on horseback armed with spears and swords),[16] and in the *Gothic War*, he pointed out how the

Byzantine cavalry, which used the bow, had the advantage over the Goths, whose archers fought on foot.[17] His strictures on Dagisthaeus, the young commander whom Justinian sent to Petra in 549, sound like the conclusions of a judicial investigating committee. Dagisthaeus laid siege to Petra and mined the walls, but then he failed to apply fire to the foundations. Had he done so, writes Procopius, the walls would have collapsed and the city would have fallen.[18] Even Belisarius' errors in strategy did not pass unnoticed. When he returned to Italy in 544 to carry on the war there, he was ill advised enough to sail to Ravenna and allowed himself to be shut up there, while the Goths had their way elsewhere in the peninsula. However, Procopius pointed out that Belisarius made this tactical blunder at the urging of another officer,[19] for in the *Wars,* he usually diverted blame from his commander by indicating that his errors arose from following bad advice from his staff, or yielding to the clamor of insubordinate soldiers.

There was also a tendency to think in strategic terms. He stressed the value of discipline in the army because it won battles. He was impatient with the subtleties of theology,[20] but he was very aware of the strategic consequences of the imperial policies on religion. He reported, without comment, that one cause of the army mutiny which broke out in Africa in 536, was that Justinian forbade the Arian priesthood the right to administer the sacraments; he was careful to point out that over one thousand soldiers of the Arian faith were to be found in the imperial army.[21]

He spoke in the *Wars* with the voice of the military establishment, but it was an independent voice. He distributed praise and blame judiciously, and even Belisarius was not entirely above reproach, though he was handled gently. Procopius was willing to praise ability even in those officers whom he criticized openly or by implication. In the *Gothic War,* he described the friction between Belisarius and John, the nephew of Vitalian, and noted how John refused to carry out his commander's orders; yet he characterized John as "both daring and self-reliant to the greatest degree, and without hesitation in the face of danger."[22] He was loud in his criticism of Bessas, who commanded the garrison in Rome when the Goths besieged it for the second time in 545–46,[23] and succeeded in capturing it. He claimed that the chief interest of Bessas had been to make money by selling grain, which he had horded, to the starving civilians at inflated prices. Yet later, when Procopius came to write his eighth book, his attitude had mellowed. He described how Bessas was appointed commander in Lazica after Dagisthaeus' failure there; and though he was by then a very old man, he led a courageous attack on Petra and took it by storm.[24] The harsh remarks about Bessas' conduct in Rome were forgotten. Now Procopius said simply that Bessas had suffered bad luck when Rome fell to the Goths, but at Petra, his luck had changed. There is not a word about his profiteering. At any rate, most of the officers in Justinian's service were guilty of offenses in private and public life, as Procopius wrote in his eighth book, in a moment of startling candor.[25]

There was, however, one commander for whom Procopius had only praise: the emperor's cousin, Germanus. Sent to Africa to suppress the mutiny led by Stotzas, he acted with an intelligence and firmness which Procopius clearly admired. We hear him addressing the imperial troops with words which are a faint echo of those Alexander the Great once used, when his Macedonians rebelled against his policies:

Fellow soldiers, you have nothing for which you can rightly blame the emperor, nor any charge to lay against him for what he has done to you, and this, not any of you, I think, could deny. For he took you as you came out of the fields with your duffel-bags and the single little coat you had on, and brought you to Byzantium, and made you into such important people that now the future of the Roman state depends on you. And you know perfectly well that it has been his fortune not only to be outrageously insulted, but to suffer the most terrible of all things at your hands. . . . It is reasonable, therefore, that you should learn loyalty over again, and correct your past foolishness.[26]

Alexander's words, reminding his men of what his father, Philip, had done for them, had had a similar flavor. Was the reminiscence deliberate?

Germanus reappeared at Antioch in 540, the year that Chosroes broke the "Endless Peace" and invaded the empire. His conduct was scarcely heroic. Yet, in Procopius' description of how Chosroes sacked Antioch, no blame was attached to Germanus. Professor Glanville Downey has argued that Procopius deliberately whitewashed Germanus' record,[27] and probably he is right. For, according to Procopius, Germanus waited at Antioch for reinforcements from the capital. None came. Thereupon he decided it would be better to evacuate the city, since he could not defend it with the forces he had, and he felt that his presence in Antioch might actually induce Chosroes to attack, for it would be a great thing to capture a cousin of the emperor. So he left Antioch to its fate. However, the blame for the sack was diverted from Germanus and fell, instead, by implication on whoever failed to send reinforcements.[28]

Finally, in 550, Justinian appointed Germanus as commander of the war against the Goths and gave him a small army, but a great deal of money with which to recruit soldiers. "Then," wrote Procopius, "a high ambition took hold of Germanus to overthrow the Gothic kingdom, so that he might have the fortune to recover for the Roman empire both Libya and Italy."[29] His preparations included a politic marriage to Matasuntha, the granddaughter of Theodoric, and so, presumably, he was aiming not to extirpate the Goths, as Narses did later, but to turn them into loyal subjects of the empire. But in the autumn of 550, he died. Procopius writes:

Thus did Germanus pass away suddenly, a man who was brave and remarkably energetic, in war a splendid general, independent, and resourceful in action, and in peace and prosperity, one who knew well how to guard the laws and established order of the state with all firmness. . . . As far as his power permitted, he would not allow any offence against the customary usage of the palaces.[30]

Even in the *Secret History,* Procopius' attitude toward Germanus remained unchanged. There he recorded how Theodora persecuted Germanus' family,[31] a fact which may have warmed Procopius toward him. But the real reason for Procopius' favor was that Germanus was thoroughly professional in war: resourceful, energetic, brave, and willing to act independently when necessary, while in peace he upheld the established laws, and was no innovator. He championed "the customary usages of the Palace" when, as the *Secret History* informs us, Justinian and Theodora were overturning them. Close familiarity with Belisarius had left him a very tarnished hero, but Germanus remained high in Procopius' regard until the end. Of course, we should add that his acquaintance with Germanus must have been more superficial.

Only Germanus survived Procopius' disillusion intact, and the disillusion came early. In 533, there was guarded optimism as the Byzantine fleet sailed off against the Vandal kingdom. The next year, some of Belisarius' officers were already trying to poison the emperor's mind against their commander, but Justinian's reaction was statesmanlike; he allowed Belisarius himself to make the choice to return to Constantinople, and when he did return, he granted him a triumph. Yet, Procopius clearly believed that it had been a mistake not to keep Belisarius in command of Libya a little longer.

There is still a spirit of high adventure in his prose as he described the first siege of Rome in 536-37. A handful of men, outnumbered fifty to one, held the city for over a year in an epic struggle. But there are hints of criticism. With just three hundred men, Belisarius could have held the Portus Traiani, and made it easier to supply the beleaguered city, but the men could not be spared. Reinforcements came slowly, and even the hero of the siege, Belisarius, committed an "unholy act": he put his officer Constantinus to death. After the siege was over, Procopius seemed to have acquired a new awareness of the cost of war in terms of human distress.

But the note of disillusion did not become insistent until 540, when Chosroes reopened the Persian War. As Procopius described the sack of Antioch in that year, he burst out bitterly,

But I grow dizzy when I write of such suffering, and pass on to future times its memory, for I cannot understand why it is the will of God to exalt on high the fortunes of a man or a place, and then cast them down for no cause that we can see. For it is not right to say that with Him all things are not done according to reason [*kata logon*], though He then endured seeing Antioch brought to the ground at the hands of a most unholy man. . . .[32]

It was an outburst at once bewildered and angry. The Christian God should act according to reason, that is, according to the *Logos* or Divine Reason, and the vicegerent of God, the emperor, was, by virtue of his position, the friend of the *Logos*. Yet God allowed an evil man like Chosroes to sack Antioch.

Even now, the painful impression which the fall of Antioch made on Procopius strikes the reader forcibly. The tribulations of the city of Rome never evoked such a depth of feeling from him, and somehow, his faith in the orderly arrangement between heaven and the

Byzantine Empire was shaken. In any case, as he looked back on the year 540, it must have struck him as a turning point. The Persians overran the East, and Belisarius won a false victory in Italy, which only cleared the stage for a more deadly struggle. In 542, the plague struck Constantinople; in 544, Belisarius went to fight a second campaign against the Goths which ended ingloriously, for God had decided that he should fail, and it made no difference how clever his strategy was. Procopius remarked gloomily, "I think that a man who is marked for bad luck has no ability to plan wisely, for he has lost his understanding and feeling for truth because he must needs suffer ill."[33] For all that, Procopius was openly critical of the conduct of the Byzantine officers and administrators in Italy in the decade after the fall of Ravenna.[34] The soldiers were insubordinate; their pay was in arrears. (Procopius drew the obvious connection between these two facts.) And, in contrast, the new king of the Goths, Totila, displayed the characteristics of a true leader. Without being exact about statistics, Procopius gave the impression that the Byzantine forces in Italy were heavily outnumbered. But he avoided direct criticism of Justinian, though he did go so far as to hint that he neglected the war for other, unnamed business.[35]

In the eighth book, Procopius was both more bitter and more reckless. During the six years that had intervened since the publication of the first seven books, Procopius seemed to have lost some of his caution and to have become a more independent critic. Justinian had been negligent[36]; now he states it openly. The peace which ended the war with Persia had been shameful. The Vandal War resulted in the depopulation and impoverishment of Libya, and when the Goths in Italy were crushed, it was only with a vastly superior army. Procopius treated Narses' victory at Busta Gallorum with a conspicuous lack of rejoicing. So ended the renewal of the empire. Justinian's efforts had been crowned with a success of sorts, but the gloomy outlook of Procopius only grew darker. The fortune of the empire had somehow gone awry.

This is the evidence of the *Wars* for Procopius' intellectual odyssey. It would indicate that, early in his career, he accepted the regime, not perhaps with outright enthusiasm, but without bitterness. His attitude was that of professional soldier whose military objectives were selected for him by the emperor, and the virtues which he admired in a commander were those we might expect a good soldier to like. When his attitude changed, the evidence suggests that the change was caused not merely by disillusion with the chiefs of staff and perhaps personal disappointment but also by religious doubts. God was no longer beneficent; He allowed Antioch to fall, which was beyond theological explanation, and He ordained that Belisarius should fail in his second campaign against the Goths. Procopius did not overtly draw the conclusion that the world was suffering from the anger of God, and yet this implication is latent.

If we could date the year when Procopius' attitude changed, the *History of the Wars* would suggest that it was 540, the year that Antioch fell. However, the disillusion did not take place overnight, and the highly educated bureaucrat who watched the Byzantine troops enter Ravenna in 540 was already a more troubled man than he was when he set forth on the Vandal expedition. We may suspect that the plague which Procopius witnessed in Constantinople also contributed to his changed outlook. But we cannot tell, for when Procopius described the plague, he wore his Thucydidean mask.

II   *The Outlook in the Secret History*

Even in his gloomier moments, the Procopius of the *Wars* had never lost the attitude of a military professional. In the *Secret History,* this attitude has vanished entirely. The causes of historical events had become backroom deals, and warfare a matter of intrigue. When generals advanced or retreated, they did so for personal, not for strategic, reasons, although admittedly Procopius had not become entirely blind to military considerations. To cite an instance I have already pointed out, when Belisarius retired from Sisauranon on the Persian front in 541 and threw away a chance to march on to the Persian capital (if we are to believe the *Secret History*), Procopius did not deny that there were strategic reasons for his action, but they were not really the ones that mattered. However, he was no longer greatly interested in the wars of Justinian, except where they provided examples of villainy. The secret historian made no effort to distinguish rumor and half-truth from fact; everything was grist for his mill so long as it was maleficent.

Yet the Procopius who had had doubts about the *Logos* of God when Antioch fell had now come to a kind of understanding. The reason for the evil fortune of the empire was the emperor, who should have been the friend of the *Logos,* had he been a true *basileus.* But Justinian was not.

The classical mask which Procopius assumed in his *Wars* has misled modern historians from Gibbon on into thinking that he was a product of the eighteenth-century Enlightenment who had somehow wandered into the Byzantine world.[37] In fact, he was well-versed in theology, and he could even consider writing an ecclesiastical history, which required something more than passing knowledge of the Christian authors. The belief that an Antichrist would come in the last days went back to the Apocalypse of Saint John, and in the fourth century, Lactantius had described his coming thus:

> Then a most powerful enemy . . . shall be constituted prince of all. He shall harass the world with an intolerable rule; shall mingle things divine and human; shall contrive things impious to relate, and detestable, shall meditate new designs in his breast, that he may establish the government for himself: he will change the laws, and appoint his own; he will contaminate, plunder, spoil and put to death. And, at length, the name being changed and the seat of government being transferred, confusion and disturbance of mankind will follow. Then, in truth, a detestable and abominable time shall come, in which life shall be pleasant for none of men.
> Cities shall be utterly overthrown, and shall perish, not only by fire and the sword, but also by continual earthquakes and overflowings of waters, and by frequent diseases and repeated famines. For the atmosphere will be tainted, and become corrupt and pestilential. . . .[38]

This was the Antichrist as foretold by Lactantius. The emperor in the *Secret History* also changed laws, meditated new designs, and harassed the world with war, earthquake, and plague. His age was a "detestable and abominable time," when life was pleasant for no one, though Procopius' immediate interest was the lack of pleasure felt by his own class.

When Procopius died, we must, believe that there were some trusted friends who saw to it that the *Secret History* survived. We cannot say who these friends were; however, we should note that the message of the *Secret History* was not rebellion. The only hint of that is the intimation that Belisarius' friends expected him to lead a rebellion about 544, but he disappointed them. Otherwise, the tone is one of bitter resignation. The conclusion of the *Secret History* looked forward to the death of Justinian, but it was to his natural death. There was no suggestion that the Antichrist might be overthrown by violent revolution, and it is clear that Procopius, and no doubt, his "fellow conspirators" too, were terribly afraid of being discovered and denounced.

The *Secret History* is no call to revolt, but still, its tone of protest is reminiscent of one of the great philosophical traditions of the ancient world, of Cynicism. The Cynics had cultivated outspokenness and freedom of speech and had a tradition of opposing tyrants. They liked to turn conventional concepts upside down, and they developed a serio-comic manner of writing, some traces of which we may recognize in the *Secret History,* which has its titillating passages. The Cynic school had revived in the first century A.D.; and under Vespasian (A.D. 69–79), Rome and the Orient were full of Cynic beggar philosophers who were fond of comparing their ideal of the philosopher-king with the actual conduct of the Roman emperors.

The secret historian also opposed a tyrant. By turning the conventional concept of the sacerdotal *basileus* inside out, he emerged with the picture of Justinian as prince of the devils. Yet there was no place for freedom of speech in Justinian's Byzantium[39]—not, at least, among the senators. Procopius confined his outspokenness to an unpublished pamphlet, whose existence can have been known only by a trusted few.

CHAPTER 6

Christianity and Paganism in Procopius

THERE is an apparent ambiguity in Procopius' attitude toward religion which lures the modern historian into making guesses about what his personal beliefs may have been. Brought up on history books which tell how the Byzantine world was racked with theological dispute over the essence of Christ, we are not prepared to find a contemporary of Justinian who states that he thinks it absurd to want to know the nature of God. Yet Procopius does say this in his *History of the Wars,* even with a touch of disdain, although he was well aware that the emperor himself devoted an enormous amount of energy to just this absurdity. Of course, Procopius must have maintained a façade of orthodoxy, for otherwise the law would have barred him from a career in the imperial bureaucracy. The fact that he was appointed legal secretary to a high-ranking general guarantees that his record was clear. Yet a long series of distinguished historians have suspected that his orthodoxy was only skin deep.

Edward Gibbon thought that he betrayed "occasional conformity, with a secret attachment to Paganism and Philosophy," and the best of Gibbon's many editors, J. B. Bury, called him at core a pagan. Without going quite so far, a whole series of modern scholars have decided that he was a skeptic, or a deist, or, as Berthold Rubin has suggested, an agnostic with a fatalist view of the world, whose outlook can be compared with Pyrrhonism, or with Spencer and Huxley, if we want to take modern examples. In general, however, the verdict of Procopian scholars has not been greatly different from

Gibbon's. It is that Procopius was a superficial Christian whose thought processes still worked within a pagan framework. Two recent studies are worth citing, for they sum up the conventional wisdom now on the subject. The first, by Professor Glanville Downey, points out that there are parallels between Procopius and Saint Augustine on the one hand, and between Procopius and the last pagan emperor, Julian the Apostate, on the other. He concludes, "Procopius may well have been a Christian of the independent and skeptical sort, which seems to have existed, apparently tolerated, or at least not seriously molested, by the orthodox believers."

The second study, by Averil Cameron, concludes that Procopius was "not only a Christian but a conventional one." Yet, she too indicates that elements of pagan thought and Christianity sit side by side in Procopius' works, apparently unreconciled.[1]

Yet, we cannot read the *Secret History* without thinking that, if Procopius was a skeptic as most scholars agree, he was not a gentle one. A few moderns have wondered if the visceral hatred displayed in that work might not be *odium theologicum*: the bitterness of a religious fanatic. Could Procopius, perhaps, have been a heretic? This is a possibility which deserves more attention than it has yet received, but unfortunately, Procopius has not provided us with enough evidence to come to much more than a tentative conclusion. Some scholars have wondered if his racial origins might have had some bearing on his outlook, if only we could discover what they were. Harold Nicholson referred to him once as "the Jew from Caesarea"; Berthold Rubin thought it possible that he was a Jew but preferred to make him a Syrian, and another Procopian scholar has suggested that he was a Samaritan.[2] Procopius does tell us about Samaritans living in Caesarea, some of whom pretended to adopt Christianity in order to escape the penalties which Justinian enacted against them, and perhaps Procopius was one of these; yet, if so, he gives us no clue.

In any case, there is no need to invoke racial origins or religious fanaticism to account for the bitterness expressed in the *Secret History*. Procopius disapproved of the imperial policies on religion, but they did not rouse such deep emotions as Justinian's innovations which affected the senatorial class. We may abandon the problem of his race without further ado; whatever it was (probably mixed: we have already noted that he could read Syriac), he seems to have been thoroughly assimilated into the Greek cultural traditions as they existed in the sixth century A.D. But the problem of his religious outlook deserves further examination. We must not expect a systematic philosophy of history from him, for, contrary to Gibbon's dictum, he was no philosopher. Yet he appears to impose pagan concepts of historical causation on the Christian world in a way that must arouse uneasiness about his orthodoxy.

Part of the ambiguity stems from the literary mask which he assumed. His language is classical Attic, and he compromises only reluctantly with his standards. He will even overcorrect. To give an instance: the dual number was obsolete in Periclean Athens, but it lives again in the pages of Procopius. Yet many readers wonder when they find these standards applied to Christian terminology. To be sure, he does refer to Jesus once as the Son of God and describes the miracles he performed while on earth without a hint of skepticism.[3] But his usual manner of referring to God is impersonal and anonymous; it sounds better suited to Socrates than to a sixth-century Byzantine Christian. And what are we to make of a writer who avoids calling a church a church (*ekklesia*) or a bishop a bishop (*episkopos*) but uses circumlocutions such as, "a shrine . . . which they call an *ekklesia*" or "one of the priests whom they call bishops."[4] Even Pope Silverius in Rome is labeled "the priest of the city" at one point, and at another, "high priest of the city,"[5] as if he occupied a position like the priesthood of the deified Alexander in Alexandria. In the *Buildings,* we find that Procopius is somewhat more willing to use contemporary terminology for churches and monasteries, but this work presented him with a special problem. Churches and monasteries bulked large in Justinian's building program, and it was difficult to describe them without naming them, except by circumlocutions. Even so, Procopius classicized as best he could.

Yet we have already noted this point of style, and seen that it is by no means just Christian terminology which is singled out for this treatment. We must remember that Procopius' classical mask is purely literary, and we can infer nothing from it about his personal beliefs. But he gives us more authentic clues about his religious outlook, and we should examine these.

I   *The Orthodox Outlook*

Procopius stated that attempting to learn the nature of God was absurd, but he claimed to speak as one who had examined all the arguments. "I am fully aware of the disputed points, but I shall by no means go into them. For I think it some kind of senseless foolishness to investigate what sort of thing the nature of God is. For I believe that mankind cannot understand human affairs accurately, much less those questions which bear on the nature of God."6 Rather to our surprise, in the last book of the *Wars,* Procopius announced his intention of writing a treatise on the "matters over which the Christians fight among themselves,"7 and again in *Secret History,* he appeared to repeat the promise, "For the measures which he [Justinian] took concerning the Christians will be described by me in the following narrative."8 But he does not fulfill this promise in the *Secret History,* and, as far as we know, he never wrote a separate work on theological disputes.

However, we should note that the *Secret History* does devote a section to what Procopius seemed to regard as a separate subject, the "many rejected beliefs of the Christians which they are accustomed to call 'heresies.' "9 Under this heading of "rejected beliefs," he listed Montanism, Sabbatianism, Arianism, and "all others by which the opinions of men are wont to wander from the truth." Samaritanism and paganism also fall into this category. But there was one important omission, which, unlike the others which Procopius did mention, was anything but a spent force: Monophysitism. Apparently, in Procopius' mind, Monophysitism was a disputed doctrine, but not a rejected one, and hence, presumably, not a heresy.

It is hard to say how much we should infer from this observation. As a native of Palestine, Procopius must have been very aware of the Monophysite strength in the East, where the Monophysite church was being organized during his lifetime. Yet, if he had had any personal sympathy for Monophysitism, we should have expected him to mete out kinder treatment to the empress Theodora. Instead, he accused Theodora and Justinian of actually creating strife by pretending to take opposing theological positions, the one championing the Monophysites, the other enforcing Orthodoxy. He seems to have imagined that somehow, this rent in the fabric of Christendom could have been mended if the imperial couple had presented a firm, united front.

The disapproval which Procopius voiced against Justinian's religious policies was based simply on political grounds. He saw the problem through the eyes of a property holder and a taxpayer. For the legal disabilities which Justinian laid on heretics, pagans, and Samaritans were many; they were excluded from public office, they could name as their heirs only persons of the orthodox faith, and they were excluded from the legal profession. One law ordered Samaritan synagogues destroyed; another forbade pagans to become teachers.[10] Yet of all these, Procopius singled out for special mention the one measure which struck him as particularly heinous: heretics were forbidden to hand on their property by will to their families.[11] Tampering with the laws of inheritance was persecution indeed.

Procopius also emphasized the economic consequenes of Justinian's measures to enforce orthodoxy. They drove the Samaritans in Palestine to revolt, and, according to Procopius' estimate, one hundred thousand died in the struggle. As a result, the land, which was "the most fruitful in the whole world" (here we have the voice of a native), was denuded of its Samaritan farmers, and this had a very serious consequence for the Christian landholders. They became responsible for the taxes on the abandoned farms, even though they derived no income from them.[12] Procopius preferred tolerant religious policies, but not necessarily, it seems, for ideological reasons. Toleration was good for business.

But we must do Procopius justice. Justinian's muscular orthodoxy not only had evil consequences for the landholders, but it offended Procopius' common sense and his idea of propriety. The emperor, in his determination to impose one single belief on everyone, created senseless destruction.[13] Procopius did not appear to have disapproved so much of Justinian's theological position (he calls it at one point, with apparent approbation, a "firm belief"),[14] as of his relentless determination to impose it on others. Yet, the fanatic resistance of the heretics was equally senseless. Procopius thought that the Montanists, who shut themselves up in their churches and set fire to them rather than accept orthodoxy, were unreasonable creatures,[15] and he approved of those urbanized Samaritans in Caesarea who went through the pretense of becoming Christians rather than suffer persecution.[16]

The Jews are mentioned only once in the *Secret History*. Procopius noted that Justinian would not allow them to celebrate the Passover when it fell before Easter: that is, he forced them to observe the Lenten season.[17] Procopius took the view that this was an unwarranted breach of custom, but his indignation was muted compared to that aroused by Justinian's other crimes. The *History of the Wars* gives little to indicate what Procopius' attitude toward the Jews may have been. The Jews in Naples supported the Ostrogoths when Belisarius laid siege to the city in 536, and when the Byzantines took it by storm, they met stubborn resistance from a group of Jewish soldiers who guarded one section of the wall.[18] Procopius mentioned these facts without drawing what, to the modern historian, is the obvious conclusion: the Jews preferred Ostrogothic to Byzantine rule because it was more tolerant. However, perhaps Procopius intended his readers to infer this, but if so, he was only pointing out the military consequences of imperial policy toward religious dissidents. The evidence for making Procopius a Jew himself amounts to nothing.[19]

There is no reason to think that Procopius was anything but an orthodox Christian whose outlook had been tempered a little by a good classical education. Moreover, he was a conservative opposed to change, particularly when the changes had evil political consequences, and Justinian's measures enforcing orthodoxy did represent a change from the usages of the past. Previously, for instance, Judaism and Samaritanism had been "permitted religions" (*religiones licitae*) under Roman law. Yet Procopius' shafts were not aimed at Justinian's religious beliefs (he thought the emperor was a hypocrite, but that was a different matter), but rather at the methods he used to force them on others. Procopius and Justinian had two divergent concepts of statesmanship. The emperor was an ideologist; Procopius, a pragmatist.

But can we call Procopius a skeptic on matters of Christian faith? He has often been called one, and it is easy to find evidence for his skepticism on matters which have nothing to do with Christianity. For instance, he expressed doubts about the Sibylline oracles, which he claimed to have examined. But it is hard to discover any trace of disbelief in Christian dogma. He evidently accepted miracles. One of his entertaining anecdotes in the *Persian War* concerned a hermit in Syria, Jacob by name, who devoted his life to prayer and contemplation. A band of White Huns came upon the hermit and raised their bows to shoot him, but as they did so, their hands became paralyzed and they could do nothing. King Cabades of Persia came to see what had happened, and when he learned the truth, he begged Jacob to forgive the Huns. When he forgave them, the paralysis disappeared.[20] Procopius related this tale with all the wide-eyed naïveté with which Herodotus could retail similar anecdotes. There is no trace of skepticism.

Let us take another example which is somewhat better.[21] In A.D. 539, a comet appeared which Procopius duly described. Wise men disagreed about the meaning of this phenomenon, but Procopius himself declined to take sides, stating: "I am putting down only what happened to occur, and I let everyone judge as he wishes from the outcome of events." What happened was, first, that a horde of Huns crossed the Danube and ravaged the country as far south as Thermopylae in Greece. Then, shortly afterward, the Persians broke the "Endless Peace" and launched the attack which culminated in the sack of Antioch. We can assume that Procopius accepted portents; at least, his presentation of the evidence would not encourage us to believe that he was skeptical about them.

The *Buildings* is a poor witness for Procopius' private beliefs, though we may take it as evidence of the attitudes he advertised to the public. It retails the story of how Justinian suffered from a sore on his knee which would not heal until he was cured by a relic discovered in the foundation of the church of the martyr Eirene.[22] No skepticism there. However, in the *Secret History,* if anywhere, we should expect to find evidence of disbelief in Christian faith and morals, and yet, it yields nothing. On the contrary, the secret historian took a moral tone; he berated his victims when they broke their promises and professed to find their private lives offensive to a good Christian. He would not name Theodora's profession before she was married, he wrote, because God would not be merciful to a man who uttered such a name.[23] Another example involved Belisarius. When he was sent against the Persians in 542, he was "guilty of cowardice."[24] The reason was that he had broken his word to his stepson Photius, and thereafter he found that God was hostile, "as one would expect." In addition, the *Secret History* reveals a Procopius who believed in demonology. He condemned witchcraft and sorcery, but he accepted the power of witches; he even speculated that Antonina practiced witchcraft on her husband.[25]

However, as we have already noted a number of times, Procopius was fond of relating a story or a rumor, and then adding, in Herodotean fashion, that he could not say whether or not it was accurate. This gentle skepticism was part of his classical mask, and it never touched matters of Christian faith or morals. As far as we can test it, the orthodoxy which Procopius professed was sincere enough. If he condemned Justinian's religious policies, it was because they upset the established order, wiped out rights which the law had recognized in the past, and resulted in hardship for all and rebellion. Procopius' tolerance was traditionalist, and Justinian's bigotry revolutionary. Perhaps this overstates the case, but in its main essentials, it is true.

II   *Fate, Chance, and God*

More than anything else, it has been Procopius' idea of historical causation which has given him his reputation as a semipagan. Again and again in the *History of the Wars of Justinian,* the goddess Fortune, *Tyche,* appears to manipulate the actors who participate in the events described. *Tyche* had been a powerful deity in the pagan world. In the first century A.D., Pliny the Elder had paid tribute to her universality in a passage in his *Natural History*[26]: everyone called upon her, he wrote, blamed her if things went wrong and praised her if they went well. She was inconstant, blind, and irrational. Plutarch had written a brief essay on fortune, beginning with a quotation from the tragic poet Chaeremon: "The affairs of men are governed by chance, not good judgment." However, Plutarch himself preferred to save a place for good judgment.

Tyche, the concept of the incalculable in history, entered the traditions of classical historiography with Thucydides. For Thucydides, *tyche* was simply accident or coincidence, and he was too much of a determinist to allow it much scope. The concept was in the air, however, and Anaxagoras, the philosopher friend of Pericles, defined *tyche* as a cause hidden from human knowledge. The Peripatetic school, which stemmed from Aristotle, assigned *tyche* an important role. We have a fragment of Demetrius of Phalerum which reflects on the whims of *tyche* as she causes the rise and fall of empires. But after Thucydides, it was the historian Polybius who contributed most to the development of the concept. For him, tyche had two meanings. At one extreme, it was unforeseeable accident, much as it had been in Thucydides. At the other, it was a superior power which put events in order so that they gravitated toward a predestined outcome. It was "providence," or simply "manifest destiny"; for instance, as Polybius saw it, *tyche* guided events in such a way that Rome would become ruler of the world.[27]

Christian thinkers could hardly accept either variety of *tyche* into their concept of world history. The message of Saint Augustine's *City of God* is explicit: all things must be referred to divine intelligence, and this included all notions of chance, whether mere coincidence, or "manifest destiny." Human beings spoke of chance events simply because they were unable to see any reason for them. It was the imperfect vision of the beholder which gave *tyche* the appearance of power, but actually, there was no valid reason for supposing that any such irrational power was able to intervene in history.[28]

Procopius inherited the concept of *tyche* along with his classical education as part of the amalgam of Stoic, Platonist, and Aristotelian philosophy taught in the schools of the sixth century. We would expect that his classical mask would require some reference to *tyche*. Yet its role in Procopius seems to be more than a literary heritage, and we should examine a number of examples.

There is the *tyche* which acts as a force that exalts men and then brings them low for no sensible reason. The Vandal king Gelimer, besieged on Mount Papua after losing two pitched battles, requested the Byzantine commander to send him a lyre, a sponge, and a loaf of bread. With the lyre he wished to sing an ode which he had composed on his misfortunes; with the sponge he wanted to bathe his eyes which had become inflamed; and he wanted a loaf of bread because he had not seen one since the siege began. When Pharas, the Byzantine commander, received this message, he was deeply moved and lamented the *tyche* of mankind: the irrational force which exalted Gelimer to the throne of the Vandal kingdom and then, within a few months, brought him so low that he made this pitiful request.[29] However, Pharas did not relax his siege in the slightest.

This irrational *tyche* also played with the king of the Goths,

Totila. Procopius states that chance gave him good fortune for no reason and then, without any proper cause, brought him to an ignominious death after the defeat at Busta Gallorum. "But," he writes, "these matters have never been comprehensible to man, I think, nor will they ever be in the future."[30]

Tyche could be good luck as well as bad. *Tyche* arranged that Belisarius should march into Syracuse on the last day of his consulship, December 31, 535, and so he laid down his office there instead at the senate house in Constantinople.[31] *Tyche* could also show a failing for symmetrical patterns in history for no particular reason. The careers of the two officers, Bessas and Dagisthaeus, provided good examples of this sort of thing. Bessas lost Rome to the Goths when it was besieged by Totila, but later, when he was assigned to Lazica, he recovered Petra from the Persians. Dagisthaeus suffered disgrace at Petra, but after he was released from prison and sent to Italy, he recaptured Rome. Procopius comments:

At this point in my narrative, I feel like remarking on how *tyche* makes a game of human affairs, not always visiting man in the same way, or looking on them with just eyes, but shifting about to fit the time and place. She plays a kind of childish sport with them, raising and lowering the merits of the poor wretches to fit the time, place, or circumstance. So Bessas, who previously lost Rome, not much later recovered Petra in Lazica for the Romans, while on the other hand Dagisthaeus, who had let Petra slip to the enemy, won back Rome in short order for the emperor. But these things have been since the beginning, and always will be, as long as the same *tyche* has power over men.[32]

Yet even when *tyche* was favorable, she was always untrustworthy. This thought occurred to Procopius even in the midst of one of his great victory scenes, when Belisarius and his officers feasted in Gelimer's palace after their triumphal entry into Carthage. One could see *tyche* in all her glory, Procopius remarked, showing that everything is hers, and that nothing is in the possession of man.[33] It was a faintly chilling thought at that glorious moment.

Occasionally, Procopius indicated that a man who is truly wise governs his affairs in such a way as to give *tyche* the smallest scope for operation. During the Nika revolt, one of the senators, whom Procopius cast as a stock "wise-counsellor" figure, advised the mob not to make war on Justinian, nor to look for a swift decision, for wars and swift decisions fell under the governance of *tyche*. In other words, we give *tyche* an opening when we embark on an event whose outcome is unpredictable. We find even Belisarius warning his men of this truth, when they clamored to be led into battle at Callinicum: the wiser course for the soldiers was to avoid battle and opt for a predictable outcome rather than submit to a force which they could not control. However, the soldiers preferred to fight the Persian army and lost.[34]

The chief characteristic of *tyche* was that no human being could predict it. Yet it could work in conjunction with a predestined conclusion. To cite an example: a Byzantine commandant in the fortress of Petra, John by name, was holding out bravely against Persian attack when, "by some chance," he was hit in the neck by an arrow and died. "For," explained Procopius, "it was fated that Petra be captured by Chosroes."[35] Elsewhere his views are even more explicit. Before Belisarius' first great victory in Libya at the tenth milestone outside Carthage, Procopius paused to reflect on the ways of heaven and of mankind,

But as for me, in the course of this battle, I was moved to wonder at the ways of God and of men, for I saw that God, who views from afar off what will be, traces out the way He thinks it best that events conclude, but whether men make errors, or formulate plans to fit their needs, they are unaware if they have failed (if that is what happens) or if they have been successful. God's purpose is to make a path for *tyche,* and she presses on relentlessly towards the preordained conclusion.[36]

If Saint Augustine could have done the impossible and read proofs of Procopius' *History of the Wars,* I think he might have nodded with approval when he encountered this sentiment.

The *Secret History* is equally to the point. We have a revealing comment on the reason why Belisarius was so unlucky in his second campaign in Italy. His failure against Totila was actually evidence of the wrath of God:

Thus there is no doubt that human affairs are governed, not by counsels of men but by the power of God, although men usually call this *tyche,* for they do not know why events turn out the way they do.

For the name *tyche* is customarily applied to whatever appears irrational. But let every man hold the opinion he likes about these matters.[37]

But though Procopius invites us to think as we please, his own opinion is clear, that the power of God is behind events which happen seemingly by chance.

Upon occasion, we have Procopius commenting on how fate operated forcefully behind apparent free will. In describing how Belisarius stormed Naples in 536, he remarked that it was not fated for the Neapolitans to become subjects of the emperor without chastisement. Nor did they. When the Byzantine troops entered the city, they ran amok and killed and plundered indiscriminately.[38] Likewise, Hypatius, whom the mob made emperor during the Nika revolt, was fated to suffer evil.[39] As Procopius related the story, he was raised to his dangerous position by a concatenation of events over which he had no control; and after the revolt was suppressed, he was executed. And to give a final example, predestination in human affairs struck Procopius most forcibly as he watched the Byzantine army march into Ravenna, after Wittigis had capitulated. "When I saw the entrance of this army into Ravenna, I considered how actions are not concluded by valor, multitudes or human virtues, but that some spirit steers the wits and judgements of men thither, where nothing can hinder the preordained conclusion."[40]

Behind historical action was the will of God. Yet, however paradoxical it may seem, it is clear that Procopius' concept of predestination left a certain amount of scope for human manipulation. Totila, who rallied the Goths after Wittigis' defeat, followed a careful policy of showing moderation and kindness to the native Italians. When the Goths complained, he told them that *tyche* was governed according to the life of each individual. An unjust person could not hope to win glory in battle.[41] Thus good luck was the reward of virtue and intelligence. Certainly, bad luck could result from sin. The *Secret History* demonstrates, as we have seen, that *tyche* turned against Belisarius after he broke his oath to his stepson Photius. God helped the just; this is very nearly a commonplace in the speeches which Procopius put into the mouths of the actors in his history. When Belisarius spoke to his army before battle with the Vandals, he told it that the Byzantines had justice on their side, for they had come to

Africa to recover their own property. "For the alliance of God," he reminded his men, "follows naturally those who put justice forward."[42]

It is significant that Procopius put this sentiment into a speech. It expressed a human view of how *tyche* should operate: it should reward virtue and punish sin, and Procopius appears to have thought that the intelligent man would conduct himself as if *tyche* did work on this principle. But his history provides little evidence that it actually did so. *Tyche* might punish sin and reward justice and intelligence; for instance, Totila enjoyed good fortune in the short run. When Procopius published his first seven books of the *Wars,* it may have seemed that *tyche* had made him her permanent favorite. Yet, when he wrote Book VIII, he knew how Totila's career had ended. As he described Totila's final scene at Busta Gallorum, he concluded that *tyche* had been playing with him after all.

When God determined predestined ends, He took into consideration factors which human wisdom could not. He might wish to punish sin (on the whole, Procopius appeared to find this easier to accept than that God rewarded virtue) but He chose the time and place. We can find this fact illustrated in a story from the *Vandal War* which relates how the usurper Gontharis was murdered. The assassins were a group of loyal Armenian soldiers led by one Artabanes, and the first blow to be struck at Gontharis as he sat at banquet was to be given by one of his bodyguards, Artasires. Before the attempt took place, Artasires delivered himself of the following speech: "I hope to undertake this attempt without hesitating, and to touch the body of Gontharis with this sword here, but as for what will happen, I cannot say if God in His anger against the tyrant will help me with this daring deed, or if He will exact vengeance for some sin of mine, and stand in my way and block me. . . ."[43] Artasires believed that God punished sin, but he had no way of telling what particular sin He might choose to punish at any one time. If God punished Gontharis, the plot would be successful. But if He chose this moment to reward Artasires for some past misdemeanor, the result would be quite the opposite. Human intelligence could not fathom the purpose of God.

The most significant passage in the *Wars,* which affirmed the tenet that there was a rationale, the *logos* of God behind history, was one which dealt with a catastrophe that bewildered Procopius. We have already noted his emotional reaction to the fall of Antioch. He could make no sense of it, for Chosroes was an evil man, who had broken the "Endless Peace," thereby making a public display of his faithlessness. Yet, God let Antioch fall to him; there had even been portents of the disaster, if men and interpreted them rightly. But He must have had a purpose. Even here, Procopius stated flatly that it was wrong to think that, with God, everything was not done according to reason.

His classical models would have been less bewildered, for they believed in more capricious deities. Thucydides could have treated a flood, for instance, as a mere happenstance. He left no more room for coincidence than he had to, but that much he was happy to grant. It is clear from the *Wars,* and even more, from the *Secret History,* that Procopius would do nothing of the sort. If *tyche* brought flood and plague, it was done according to a reason, which God alone might know, but which existed nevertheless.

On the other hand, fate in the classical world had been a power beyond the Olympian deities. Herodotus related the story of how Croesus, king of Lydia, lost his empire to Persia with the following revelatory details: Croesus had taken every precaution before he went to war. He consulted the oracle of Apollo at Delphi and received an ambiguous answer. Believing that the god was promising him victory, he went out to fight Cyrus of Persia and lost. Afterward, he sent to Delphi to reproach the oracle. But Apollo replied that it was not his fault; apart from the fact that Croesus had misinterpreted the oracle, his allotted time was up. The best that Apollo had been able to do for him was to postpone his fate for three years, but it was beyond his power to change it.[44]

The comparison with Procopius is instructive. For Procopius, the judgment of God was not immutable; God, being a Christian deity, possessed the Christian virtues and was capable of being moved by them. The Emperor Honorius had been a weak creature, and at one point in his reign, he found himself facing two revolts at the same time, which ordinarily should have brought him down. Yet, he survived, for, as Procopius remarked, "God loves to succor and give help to men who are neither clever nor able to think out any strategy of their own, provided they are not wicked, even when they have reached the depths of despair."[45] Procopius had not forgotten that God could be merciful, and He could be moved by helplessness. Fate was not blind and unchanging; it was set by the judgment of God. Yet, the concepts of Procopius and Herodotus had something in common. Both thought that fate was beyond the discernment of human intelligence.

The *Secret History* grapples with another aspect of the problem. How could Procopius account for a *tyche* which seemed to cooperate with Justinian and Theodora to bring destruction on the world? For the efforts of the imperial pair were ably seconded by earthquakes, floods, and plague; and as we have seen, Procopius' views of causation left no room for mere happenstance. The question about God's purpose which Procopius had raised at the sack of Antioch reappears in the *Secret History,* but in a larger dimension. And the *Secret History* has the answer.

If *tyche* cooperated with Justinian and Theodora in bringing destruction, it was proof that they were in league with satanic powers. If the Antichrist predicted by the Scriptures were on the throne, he might bend *tyche* to his own evil purposes. If *tyche* failed to act in any rational way, an explanation for it could be found in theological writings. The truth would be revealed eventually: "Therefore, when Justinian either departs this life, if he is human, or lays aside his earthly being, as befits a prince of devils, all who have the luck to survive so long will know the truth."[46]

III   *Conclusion*

All of this shows two things. First, there is no reason to doubt Procopius' own orthodoxy. He did not disapprove of Justinian's theological tenets, but of his measures to force them on the empire. Second, Procopius owes many of his basic concepts to pagan historical thought, but they have been brought within a teleological Christian framework.

Chance, fate, vengeance for faults committed in the past, can all be found in classical historiography. Procopius used words and phrases taken from his pagan predecessors; but in his hands, fate became God's preordained plan, chance was a cause hidden from human knowledge but governed by the power of God, and vengeance became divine punishment for sin. At the same time, Procopius' concept of predestination does not appear to rule out free will or contingency. However illogical it may be, the fact that *tyche* cooperated with a preconceived plan, fashioned according to Divine

Reason, does not seem to make it any the less "chance." But we should not be in a hurry to accuse Procopius of confusing pagan and Christian ideas. He was not a systematic thinker, but the relation of free will and chance to divine foreknowledge had occupied minds better trained in philosophy than his.

His near coeval, Boethius, whom Procopius mentions, and could even have read, although he does not say so, had grappled with the same problem in the fifth book of his *Consolation of Philosophy*; and his conclusion might have satisfied Procopius. He attempted to show that God saw all things concurrently and eternally, although they take place in the world through a succession of time, and hence for Him to foresee acts of free will does not destroy their free will or their contingency. The ever-present eternity of God's vision agrees with the future quality of our actions. These were ideas which Boethius took from the contemporary neo-Platonist philosophic school at Alexandria, and although Procopius was no philosopher, we suspect that he was a student at Gaza, which was an intellectual outpost of Alexandria. Boethius probably had no direct influence upon him. Yet it is significant that the role Procopius assigns to *tyche* agrees well with Boethius.

This comparison with Boethius does not make the case for Procopius' being a Christian any stronger. The question whether Boethius himself was a Christian when he wrote the *Consolation of Philosophy* has not yet been entirely settled. Yet, we should remember that, for many of Procopius' contemporaries, it must have seemed not at all illogical for *tyche* to operate within a Christian teleological framework. The boundaries between Christian and pagan thought had become a little blurred by the sixth century.

As for Justinian's muscular orthodoxy, and his efforts to enforce uniform belief in the empire, Procopius considered them simply bad statemanship. There is one telling aside in the *Wars*[47] where he stated his own solution to the Monophysite dispute, although he was careful not to advertise it as such. It was simply to abandon the attempt to define the nature of God, and to accept Him as completely powerful and good. What he might have said if he had written his projected work on theological issues, we do not know, but one reference from the *Buildings* leads me to suspect that its tone might not have been entirely serious.[48] Procopius here explains to his readers that the centaurs of classical mythology were the product of a childish belief which the ancients held, that there could be one animal with two natures. In its context, this passage is probably intended to add a touch of humor, but Procopius has chosen his words with care. They are reminiscent of the creed of Chalcedon, which insisted on a Christ of two natures, though they avoid parody. Yet, I think that the reminiscence was intentional. This description of the centaur was as close as Procopius could safely come to joking about beings with double natures. If it is a covert reference to the creed of Chalcedon, then its import surely is that people took the controversy over the nature of Christ far too seriously.

As far as we can see, Procopius displays a kind of "know-nothing" attitude toward the Monophysite dispute. He was probably not a strict Chalcedonian. At the same time, he was far removed from any partisan feeling for the Monophysites, and his reaction to the controversy over the nature of Christ was that it absorbed far more time and energy than it was worth. His outlook may have been partly formed by his early training, for, as I have shown earlier, he was possibly an alumnus of the school at Gaza, which held itself aloof from the theological quarreling which absorbed the energies of the intellectual world of Alexandria and Antioch. But it was also conditioned by his career, which took him from the Monophysite East to the Chalcedonian West and back again, and made him realize the political consequences of religious schism.

However, I cannot believe that many of the wrangling churchmen of the sixth century would have been willing to accept Procopius' view of the nature of God. Justinian, for all his faults, was more attuned to the theological temper of the time.

CHAPTER 7

Epilogue

THE LAST YEARS of Justinian were marked with disappointment and misfortune. The protagonists of Procopius' *Wars* and *Secret History* shuffled off the stage one by one to a variety of fates. The empress Theodora died on June 28, 548, of a disease which can now be diagnosed as cancer. Germanus, whom she hated and feared, died in 550. Had he lived longer, he might have secured the succession to the throne for one of his own sons when Justinian died, childless, fifteen years later. As it was, Justinian's successor was his nephew, Justin II, whose wife was Theodora's niece by blood relationship.

Belisarius, retired after his recall from Italy, returned to center stage one last time. In late 558, a horde of Kotrigur Huns overran the Balkans and threatened Constantinople itself. The empire was not ready for them: its fortifications were dilapidated, and the treasury was empty. (Ironically, it was at about this time that Procopius was at work on his *Buildings*.) Faced with impending disaster, Justinian once more turned to his old commander, putting him in charge of the defense. The troops available were pitifully limited, though there was a core of three hundred veterans from the campaigns in Italy. Yet, Belisarius marched out with this force, and by some masterly tactics and clever ruses, managed to drive back the Hun invaders. Then he returned to obscurity. But not for long. A new conspiracy to assassinate Justinian was uncovered in 562. The conspirators were arrested, and their confessions implicated Belisarius, who was brought to trial and placed under house arrest. His reinstatement came some seven months later, but he did not long survive it. He died in March, 565, only a few months before the emperor, and his properties were confiscated by the state. Antonina, who outlived her husband, ended her days in a convent.

Probably Procopius was already dead. It is not unlikely that he was older than his former commander and did not live to see his last humiliation. Almost certainly, he left the *Buildings* unfinished, interrupted by sickness or death; and though already there may have been copies of parts or all of it in circulation, some anonymous editor added some finishing touches and brought out an "authorized version." What happened to the *Secret History* we do not know. As I have argued, Procopius was probably composing it as he worked on his *Buildings,* and it too may be unfinished. Somehow, it survived his death, but we have no good evidence for the date when it was published. All we can say for certain is that, by the tenth century, it was in circulation, and attributed securely to Procopius.

Procopius' importance as an historical source has been recognized since the Renaissance, but his reputation as a historian has always been faintly clouded by the one quality on which he prided himself— his classical mask. The modern age places emphasis on originality in a way that Procopius would never have understood. How can we regard a historian as great when he is an obvious imitator of Herodotus and Thucydides?

However, we should make qualifications. It is immediately obvious to anyone who reads Procopius in the original Greek that he borrowed vocabulary and phraseology from both Herodotus and Thucydides, His proem to the *History of the Wars,* carefully modeled on Thucydides, immediately invites the reader to make comparisons, and there are tags and scenes taken from these two classical historians throughout the work. Yet, we should not imagine that he worked with copies of his models propped up on his desk. His style was formed by thorough training in Thucydides and Herodotus in school. No doubt, he was made to write Greek in the style of Thucydides, not unlike modern classics majors in college. In the case of Thucydides, it has been noted that he borrowed most heavily from the first book of the *Peloponnesian War,* less so, but still liberally from Books II to IV, sparsely from Book V, and not at all from the rest.[1] Perhaps in the school at Gaza it was the first four books of Thucydides which were prescribed for special attention by the students.

We should never forget that, while Procopius' classical mask may have vitiated his originality, it brought him some practical advantages too. In the first place, it gave him the convention of composing speeches and putting them in the mouths of historical characters.

These add to the dramatic element (some of Procopius' speeches seem to have only dramatic value, and nothing else), but they could also give him a vehicle for expressing views which he wanted to convey. Belisarius spoke on the value of discipline in the army; Totila emphasized the practical rewards of justice in dealing with subject peoples. Armenian envoys, addressing the king of Persia, might present the seamier side of Justinian's program to renew the Roman Empire. They accused the emperor of greedy expansionism and said that the whole world was not large enough for him.[2] Speeches could serve to establish character: Chosroes highlighted his, in words which Procopius assigned to him just after he had sacked the city of Antioch. Full of Herodotean reminiscences and references to God, they set forth Chosroes' views on the sack. He had been deeply pained by the slaughter of so many Antiochenes, but it was not his fault. His victims had not run away quickly enough, but had persisted in putting up resistance.[3] Chosroes emerges as a hypocrite who knows how to use the forms of piety to cover his villainy.

Other legacies served only to highlight the differences of the age of Procopius and the century which made his literary exemplars. For instance, he borrowed set situations, or *"topoi."* One was the Melian Dialogue in Thucydides, where the Athenians and the Melians debate the rights and wrongs of the massacre which the Athenians were about to perpetrate on Melos. Procopius' counterpart is a debate held between Belisarius and some Gothic envoys during the siege of Rome in 536–37, in the course of negotiations for an armistice.[4] The two dialogues belong to different intellectual worlds: Thucydides reflects the milieu of the Athenian Sophists, and the controversy between custom-law (*nomos*) and nature (*physis*). Procopius reflects his own training in law, and the milieu of Justinianic propaganda. First, the Goths set forth their case: they had invaded Italy in the first place at the invitation of the emperor Zeno, and therefore they could not be regarded as simple marauders; and, though Arians themselves, they had preserved religious freedom for the Catholics under their rule. Therefore it was unjust of the Byzantines to attack them. To this, the reply of Belisarius was simple: Italy was the property of the empire and hence was under Justinian's jurisdiction. The emperor could do with it as he wished. Then follow negotiations: the Goths offered to give up Sicily if they were left unmolested in Italy, and Belisarius countered by offering Britain to the Goths, which had long since been lost to the empire and was half-forgotten. But the imperial idea was still such that Belisarius assumed that Britain belonged legally to the emperor to bestow as he pleased. The Goths made another offer; Belisarius stated simply that he was without authority to act against the wishes of the emperor. The Goths thereupon said that they would negotiate directly with Justinian, and Belisarius replied that he would never block any efforts for peace.

Procopius had a lawyer's mind, and he knew history. But philosophy as it had once existed in classical Greece, had ceased to be a vital force. Whether we praise or blame Procopius for his classicizing, we should remember that it was not only he who looked to the past for models; it was the whole age. The Byzantine spirit placed no great value on creativity. Justinian himself proclaimed, as he presented his law reforms, that the man who improved something which was imperfect, deserved more praise than he who first invented it.[5] Procopius' aim was to use his exemplars as perfectly as possible. His classical Greek was carefully cultivated, and it is to his credit that he wrote a clear, strong style which compares favorably with that of the other secular historians. Yet his models never dominate him to the extent that we feel he is producing a literary exercise.

Moreover, though Procopius may have looked to the past for models, it was the rapidly changing present which molded his outlook. No doubt he shared the Christian faith of his contemporaries, but he was no fanatic. History for him operated within a teleological framework, where both fate and contingency played their roles in conducting men toward their appointed ends. Nothing would lead us to suspect that he had any systematic philosophy of history. But he was a product of the intellectual world of his times. He may have borrowed vocabulary from the Periclean age, but the substance belonged to the sixth century after Christ.

As Gibbon remarked in a brief note in his *Decline and Fall of the Roman Empire,* the literary fate of Procopius has been somewhat unlucky. He was reintroduced to the world in 1470 by Leonardo Aretino, who produced a free translation into Latin of the *Gothic War,* and published it as his own composition. The first complete Greek edition of the *History of the Wars* (including a summary of the *Buildings*) was not published until 1607. The

Secret History was discovered in the Vatican Library and published in 1623 by the librarian, Nicholas Alemmannus, with a Latin translation and notes.[6]

Immediately upon publication of the *Secret History*, Procopius was drawn into the religious and political disputes of Reformation Europe, but it cannot be said that he attracted much attention for his merits as a historian. As I have already pointed out, he suffered from the comparison with Thucydides and Herodotus which he himself invited, and also the general reputation of the Byzantine Empire weighed against him. One scholar from the late nineteenth century summed up the opinion and prejudice of the English-speaking world more succinctly, perhaps, than he intended: "Let us pause for a moment to contemplate the contrast of light and shadow afforded by this picture [the contrast between Thucydides and Procopius]. Thus we find Thucydides living in the very atmosphere of freedom, in the springtime of the world's life and thought. We behold Procopius, on the other hand, living at a time when no one dared to call his life, or even his thoughts his own, and when spies lurked in the innermost recesses of a man's household. With these changes in the political world had also come changes in the language, the religion and the national life of both the Greeks and the Romans." The same scholar concluded on a charitable note: "But when we consider the circumstances under which the latter [Procopius] wrote, the artificial character of the language, the blighting influence both of an effete civilization and a despotic system of government, we are constrained to wonder that he did as well as he did."[7]

But however much scholars slighted him, novelists, playwrights, and authors of popular histories have always found Procopius useful. Belisarius has been the subject of an opera, and Theodora provided Sarah Bernhardt with a famous role. The best of the modern historical novels based on Procopius has been Robert Graves's *Count Belisarius,* which probably outranks the same author's more famous *I, Claudius.*[8]

The renewed interest in Byzantine studies in the last eighty years has begun to bring Procopius new appreciation. The documentary evidence of the *Buildings* has been invaluable for studies in the architecture of Justinian's reign. And I notice, as a sign of the times, that a publisher who is bringing out abridged versions of "The Great Histories" in paperback, has included Procopius' works among their number.[9] Perhaps the time has come to put Procopius in his proper perspective.

Of all his classical predecessors, the one with whom he begs comparison most is the historian Polybius. Both were men of action, soldiers who saw war at firsthand, and knew what they were describing. Both belonged to periods of transition: for Polybius, the classical period of Hellenism was giving way to the Roman Empire, while for Procopius, the ancient world was yielding to the Middle Ages. Both saw chance (*tyche*) operating behind historical events, and both conceived of it as something more than mere coincidence. Polybius saw it as a kind of providence which was arranging for the rise of Rome; Procopius, a child of his own age, saw it as a force working toward an end predetermined by God. As historians, their merits are about equal. But owing to the prejudices and accidents of scholarship, Procopius has so far received far less attention.

Notes and References

The following abbreviations are used: *AJA = American Journal of Archaeology; ByzZeit = Byzantinische Zeitschrift; CQ = Classical Quarterly; CR = Classical Review; JHS = Journal of Hellenic Studies; JRS = Journal of Roman Studies; RE = Pauly-Wissowa-*Kroll-Ziegler, *Realencyclopadie der klassisichen Altertumwissenschaft* (Stuttgart, 1893 ff.); *TAPA = Transactions of the American Philological Association.*

Chapter One

1. Quoted from chapter 40 of Edward Gibbon's *The History of the Decline and Fall of the Roman Empire.* (Abridgment by D. M. Low, Harmondsworth, 1963, p. 548.)

2. G. Downey, "The Composition of Procopius' *De Aedificiis*," *TAPA,* vol. 78 (1947), pp. 171–83, esp. p. 172.

3. *Bldgs.* 1.3.1.

4. *Wars,* 7.32.9.

5. *Wars,* 2.2.6.

6. *Wars,* 5.1.29. In fact, Theodoric wore the imperial diadem, normally reserved for the emperor (F. von Lorentz, "Theoderich—nicht Justinian," *Mitteilungen des Deutschen archäologischen Instituts, Römisch Abteilung,* vol. 50 (1935), pp. 339–47, esp. pp. 342–43).

7. *SH,* 11.31. Pagans had enjoyed some degree of practical toleration before Justinian, and the enthusiasm with which he set about forcing Christianity upon them was something of a novelty; cf. D. J. Constantelos, "Paganism and the State in the Age of Justinian," *Catholic Historical Review,* vol. 50 (1964–65), pp. 372–80.

8. *Bldgs.* 6.2.16–20; 6.3.10; 6.4.12.

9. A. H. M. Jones ("Were Ancient Heresies National or Social Movements in Disguise?," *Journal of Theological Studies,* New Series, vol. 10 [1959], pp. 280–98) warns us rightly that the early Christian world thought in terms of theology rather than modern nationalism. However, these heresies soon formed focal points for anticentralist

feelings, and in the case of Monophysitism, allied itself with emerging native cultures, such as Coptic in Egypt and Syriac in the East.

10. For a description of these schools in Palestine, see Glanville Downey, "The Christian Schools in Palestine: A Chapter in Literary History," *Harvard Library Bulletin*, vol. 12 (1958), pp. 297–319. Excavations at the village of 'Auja-el-Hafir, ancient Nessana, one hundred miles southwest of Jerusalem, uncovered papyrus fragments (*P. Colt*. 1) of a Latin-Greek glossary for Virgil's *Aeneid* which had evidently been used by a schoolboy in the sixth century A.D.: evidence that Latin was taught in eastern schools at this time and that Virgil was an author studied.

11. 14. Title 1. 1. Quoted from the translation of Clyde Pharr, *The Theodosian Code and Novels and the Sirmondian Constitutions* (Princeton, 1952), p. 405.

12. *Cod. Iustinianus*, 1.5.18.

13. This point is well made by G. Downey ("Justinian's View of Christianity and the Greek Classics," *Anglican Theological Review*, vol. 40 [1958], pp. 13–22), who emphasizes Justinian's reverence for the past, and the fact that in his day, his whole program was regarded as a renewal (*renovatio*) of the *Imperium Romanum*.

14. For the style of Procopius' school, see A. and A. Cameron, "Christianity and Tradition in the Historiography of the Late Empire," *CQ*, vol. 14 (1964), pp. 316–28.

15. *Cod. Iustinianus*, 1.27.1.1–7.

16. *Nov.* 30.11.2.

17. *SH*, 6.2–3. For details, see A. A. Vasiliev, *Justin the First, An Introduction to the Epoch of Justinian the Great* (Cambridge, Mass., 1950), pp. 53–75.

18. *SH*, 6.4–9.

19. *SH*, 6.15–16.

20. *Op. cit.,* p. 546.

21. As suggested by E. Stein, *Histoire du Bas-Empire*, vol. 2. *De la disparition de l'Empire d'occident à la mort de Justinien (456-565)* (Paris-Bruxelles-Amsterdam, 1949), p. 220.

22. Speros Vryonis, *Byzantium and Europe* (London, 1967), p. 42.

23. Agathias, 5.14.

24. See E. Stein, "Introduction à l'Histoire et aux Institutions Byzantines," *Traditio*, vol. 7 (1949–51), pp. 95–168, esp. p. 138.

25. Evagrius, *Hist. Eccl.* 4.30.

26. G. Downey, "Earthquakes at Constantinople and Vicinity, 342–454. *Speculum*, vol. 30 (1955), pp. 596–600.

27. J. C. Russell, *Late Ancient and Mediaeval Population. Trans. of the American Philosophical Society*, new series, vol. 48, pt. 3 (Phil-

adelphia, 1958), p. 42. The epidemic which ravaged the Roman Empire in the reign of Marcus Aurelius may have been bubonic plague and it is even possible that this was also the plague described by Thucydides in ancient Athens. For the evidence, see E. M. Hooker, "Buboes in Thucydides," *JHS*, vol. 78 (1958), pp. 78–83. However, we cannot be certain about these identifications, whereas there is no doubt that the disease Procopius describes in bubonic plague.

28. *SH*, 23.20–21.

29. Cf. John L. Teall, "The Barbarians in Justinian's Armies," *Speculum* vol. 40 (1965), pp. 294-32.

30. Agathias, 5.13–14.

31. Ch. Diehl, *Justinien et la Civilization Byzantine au VIe Siècle* (Paris, 1901), pp. 14–15. The authenticity of the later portrait was first questioned by Von Lorentz, cited in note 6. For a brief discussion of relevant literature, see John W. Barker, *Justinian and the Later Roman Empire* (Madison, 1966), pp. 288–89.

32. *SH*, 8.12–13.

33. The arguments for the *Secret History's* authenticity are summarized by H. B. Dewing, "The secret history of Procopius of Caesarea," *TAPA*, vol. 62 (1931), pp. xl–xli. See also K. Krumbacher, *Geschichte der Byzantinischen Litteratur, von Justinien bis zum Ende des östromischen reiches (527–1453)* (Munich, 1897), pp. 231–32.

34. For Procopius' life, see W. S. Teuffel, *Studien und charakteristiken zur Griechischen und Römischen sowie zur Deutschen Literaturgeschichte* (Leipzig, 1871), pp. 191–93; J. B. Bury, *A History of the Later Roman Empire from the Death of Theodosius I to the Death of Justinian* (A.D. 395–565) (London, 1929), vol. 2, pp. 417–37; B. Rubin, "Prokopios von Kaisareia," *RE*, Bd. 23.1 cols. 273 ff.; O. Veh, *Zur Geschichtsschreibung und Weltauffassung des Prokop von Caesarea*, I. Teil (Bayreuth, 1950–51), pp. 3–7.

35. *Bldgs.* 5.7.14. J. Haury (*Procopiana*, Augsburg, 1890–91, pp. 35–36) suggested that this Procopius was the historian's father, although later he advanced the hypothesis that the historian's father was one Stephanus, a leading citizen of Caesarea and proconsul of the First Palestine, who was murdered in the Samaritan revolt of 556. The murderers were promptly punished by Justinian, and Haury suggested that, because of this, Procopius was genuinely grateful to the emperor when he wrote the *Buildings*. However, there is insufficient evidence for this hypothesis: cf. Bury, *op. cit.*, p. 420, note 1; Rubin, *op. cit., RE*, Bd. 23.1. cols. 273 ff.

36. *SH*, 11.25.

37. *Wars*, 1.5.40. Buzanta was a city in Cilicia: cf. J. Karst and C. F. Lehmann-Haupt, "Buzanta," *Klio*, vol. 26 (1933), pp. 363–67.

38. B. Rubin (*RE* Bd. 23.1. cols. 323–29) regards it as certain that Procopius knew Syriac and speculates that he knew Gothic and perhaps Persian.

39. On the schools at Gaza in the sixth century, see G. Downey, *Gaza in the Early Sixth Century* (Norman, Okla., 1963), pp. 99–116; "The Christian Schools in Palestine: A Chapter in Literary History," *Harvard Library Bulletin*, vol. 12 (1958), pp. 297–319.

I have not seen Janos Balazs, *A Gazai Iskola Thukydides tanulmanyai—Gli studi Tucididei della Scuola di Gaza* (Budapest, 1940), who argues that Gaza was a center of Thucydidean studies at this time, and that Procopius was an alumnus. See also B. Rubin, *RE*, Bd. 23, 1, col. 305.

40. For the legal education of the time, see W. W. Buckland, *A Text-Book of Roman Law from Augustus to Justinian*, 3rd ed., rev. by P. Stein (Cambridge, 1963), pp. 49–50; and H. F. Jolowicz, *Historical Introduction to the Study of Roman Law* (Cambridge, 1961), pp. 509–12. Justinian made the fifth year of legal studies standard. We should note that one of Justinian's legal reforms entailed suppressing a law school at Caesarea itself, and we should not exclude the possibility that Procopius attended lectures at this school in his youth.

41. *SH*, 30.18–20.

42. *Wars*, 1.12.24.

43. The *assessor* was a salaried official appointed by the government to assist magistrates and other officers of the state with legal advice. They were *consiliarii*, i.e., members of the *consilium* or advisory board of jurists and experts and various other fields, which every higher magistrate had at his disposal, but whose advice he was not bound to follow. See A. Berger, *Encyclopaedic Dictionary of Roman Law. Transactions of the American Philosophical Society*, new series, vol. 43, pt. 2 (1953), pp. 351, 408.

44. Cf. Diodorus, 14.8.5, who describes a council held by Dionysius the Elder, of Syracuse, when faced with a revolt of Syracusans in 404 B.C. The same story is found in Isocrates, *Archidamus*, 45, and it may go back to the historian Philistus. I owe this suggestion to my graduate student, L. J. Sanders.

45. *Wars*, 3.12.3–5.

46. *Wars*, 3.14.7–17.

47. *Wars*, 3.21.7.

48. *Wars*, 5.24.34–37.

49. *Wars*, 6.4.1–7, 19–20; 6.7.1.

50. *Wars*, 6.20.21–33. Procopius here describes the effects of the famine with clinical detail, comparable to his description of the plague in Constantinople in 542.

51. *Wars,* 5.9.2–7.
52. *Wars,* 6.29.32.
53. *Wars,* 2.22.9.
54. *SH,* 4.1–16.
55. J. Haury, *Procopiana* (Augsburg, 1890–91), pp. 8–9.
56. *Wars,* 6.15.8.
57. *Wars,* 6.5.24–27. Teuffel, *op. cit.,* p. 197, argues that "now the third year" is 545, i.e., eight years after the siege of Rome. However, Procopius is counting inclusively. The fifth year after 537 is 541, and the third year after 541 is 543, or, conceivably, early 544. Haury, *op. cit.,* pp. 5–6, attempts to use this passage to show that the *History of the Wars* was substantially complete in 545.
58. *Bldgs.* 1.1.4.
59. *Wars,* 8.25.13. There is also a reference in *SH,* 11.33, to what may be the same promise. See H. B. Dewing (trans.), *Procopius,* vol. 6, *The Anecdota or Secret History* (Cambridge, Mass., and London), pp. 362–4.
60. For this period, see A. Momigliano, "Pagan and Christian Historiography in the Fourth Century A.D.," in *The Conflict between Paganism and Christianity in the Fourth Century,* ed. Momigliano (Oxford, 1963), pp. 79–99; Wilhelm Christ, *Geschichte der Griechischen Literatur bis auf die Zeit Justinians* (Munich, 1890), pp. 663–65.
61. *SH,* 14.11; *SH,* 20.11; *Bldgs.* 3.4.16.
62. *Wars,* 2.9.14; 1.7.22.
63. *Wars,* 3.6.26. Averil Cameron ("Procopius and the Church of St. Sophia," *Harvard Theological Review,* vol. 58 [1965], pp. 161–63) comments on this peculiar circumlocution as evidence of Procopius' desire to use classical idiom. The popular designation for Hagia Sophia was simply "the great church" (*he megale ekklesia*).
64. *Wars,* 1.1.4.
65. See J. A. S. Evans, "The Dates of the *Anekdota* and the *De Aedificiis* of Procopius," "*Classical Philology,* vol. 64 (1969), pp. 30–31; also, "Procopius and the Emperor Justinian," *Canadian Historical Association. Historical Papers,* 1968, pp. 126–39.
66. Procopius may owe this geographical division of the *Wars,* to Appian: cf. Teuffel, *op. cit.,* p. 197; Krumbacher, *op. cit.,* p. 231.
67. *Cod. Justinianus,* 1.27.1.1–7.
68. *Wars,* 8.15.17. Since Justinian made the payment in a lump sum, it can be argued that this passage in Procopius means only that the eighth book was written after the treaty was renewed. Hence, the date usually cited is about 554. However, Procopius regarded these payments as yearly tribute and the most likely interpretation of the Greek would have it that Procopius was writing in 556.

69. On the river Sangarius, *Bldgs.* 5.3.8–10.
70. Theophanis, *Chronographia* (ed. C. de Boor, Leipzig. 1883), under AM6052 (A.D. 560), announces the start of this bridge, intended to replace an earlier one of wood. The same source notes under A.D. 559 two other projects described in *Bldgs.* 4.9.9–12.
71. *Bldgs.* 1.1.66–78.
72. *Bldgs.* 5.7.16.
73. *Bldgs.* 3.6.6.
74. This argument was first put forward by E. Stein, *Histoire du Bas-Empire* vol. 2 (Paris-Bruxelles-Amsterdam, 1949), p. 720, but has not been universally accepted. G. Downey (*Constantinople in the Age of Justinian* [Norman, Okla., 1960], pp. 156–59) remained faithful to the 560-date. Teuffel's discussion of the date of the *Buildings* is still valuable (*op. cit.,* p. 206), and my own conclusions are essentially in agreement with his.
75. Procopius, *Bldgs.* 1.3.1, gives grounds for believing that the plan was submitted to the emperor for approval, and the imperial assent must have been tantamount to a commission.
76. *SH,* 18.33; 23.1; 24.29; 24.33.
77. So Felix Dahn, *Prokopios von Caesarea* (Berlin, 1865), p. 52.
78. This argument was first put forward by J. Haury, *Procopiana* (Augsburg, 1890–91), pp. 9–16, and was defended by him in "Zu Prokops Geheimgeschichte," *ByzZeit,* vol. 34 (1934), pp. 10–14.
79. *SH,* 18.38 to *Bldgs.* 2.7.2–16.

Chapter Two

1. *Wars,* 1.2.1–10.
2. *Wars,* 1.11.6–30.
3. *Wars,* 1.5.1.
4. So-called from the battle cry of the rioters, *nika,* meaning "conquer!" The "Blues" and "Greens" were circus factions with political and religious overtones, the "Blues" being more aristocratic and orthodox than the "Greens." It should be remembered that these factions in the Hippodrome were the only means by which popular discontent could be expressed.
5. *Wars,* 1.24.54.
6. *Wars,* 2.1.1.
7. *Wars,* 2.22.6.
8. *Wars,* 2.28.15.
9. *Wars,* 2.28.31–37. The Persian plot was that Chosroes' ambassador, Isdigousnas, on his way to Constantinople, would lodge in Daras with five hundred attendants hand-picked for their valor, and while the Byzantine garrison was off its guard, these men would seize

the fortress. However, George, the commander of Daras, would allow Isdigousnas to enter with only twenty men. Yet, he continued to Constantinople, where he was treated with great generosity by Justinian, to Procopius' covert indignation.

10. *Wars*, 8.9.1–4.

11. *Wars*, 2.29.33–43.

12. *Wars*, 8.5.1.

13. *Wars*, 8.6.12; 8.6.15; 8.6.20.

14. During the siege of Rome in 545–46, Bessas had horded grain and sold it at inflated prices to the Romans while famine raged in the city (*Wars*, 7.17.9–16), and he failed to obey orders from Belisarius (*Wars*, 7.19.13). However, in Lazica, where he was assigned after failure in Italy, Procopius emphasizes his valor and points out, for the first, that he was over seventy years of age (*Wars*, 8.11.39–42).

15. Procopius devotes a paragraph to reporting the points of dissatisfaction which were voiced against this treaty (*Wars*, 8.15.14–18). However, he attributes these complaints to public opinion; he himself claims to be unable to say whether or not they are justified. This is a good example of Procopius using his classical mask for self-protection, for this suspension of judgment was borrowed from Herodotus.

16. *Wars*, 1.12.20–21.

17. The convention of putting speeches in the mouths of historical characters was one of the most useful legacies which Procopius inherited from the classical past. In Procopius' works, speeches in direct discourse are literary compositions, but they usually serve to convey ideas which Procopius wishes to publicize, some of them ideas which might be dangerously unpopular if they were conveyed in any other manner. A good examination of the convention is to be found in F. W. Walbank, *Speeches in Greek Historians* (Oxford, n.d.).

18. *Wars*, 1.14.17.

19. *Wars*, 1.14.21–27.

20. *Wars*, 1.18.21.

21. *SH*, 2.19–25.

22. *Wars*, 2.19.26–34.

23. *SH*, 2.25.

24. *Wars*, 2.28.18–23. The reasons were (1) possession of Lazica would secure Iberia for the Persians; (2) it would be easier for Persia to divert the Huns who neighbored Lazica against Byzantium; and (3) Lazica would be a base for Persian expansion westward along the south shore of the Black Sea.

25. *Wars*, 8.7.1–5.

26. *Wars*, 2.21.14.

27. *Wars*, 2.21.20.

28. *Wars*, 2.21.28.
29. *Wars*, 1.23.1.
30. Cf. *Wars*, 1.11.13, where a speech put in the mouth of Proclus, states that where there is innovation, there is no security.
31. *Wars*, 2.1.15.
32. *Wars*, 2.2.12.
33. *Wars*, 2.4.1.
34. *Wars*, 2.10.1–3.
35. *Wars*, 2.8.14.
36. *Wars*, 2.26.2.
37. *Wars*, 3.1.4–19.
38. *Wars*, 3.2.1.
39. *Wars*, 3.9.1.
40. *Wars*, 3.3.15.
41. Cf. B. Rubin, *Das Zeitalter Iustinians*, vol. 1 (Berlin, 1960), pp. 182–83.
42. *Wars*, 3.6.1–24.
43. Herodotus, 7.8–18. For another "set piece" in Procopius, modeled after a classical prototype, see *Wars*, 6.6.4–36. where Belisarius and a group of Ostrogothic ambassadors debate the rights and wrongs of the Byzantine invasion of Italy, in imitation of the "Melian Dialogue" of Thucydides.
44. *Wars*, 3.10.7.
45. *Wars*, 3.10.18. The nomenclature is a good example of Procopius' literary embarrassment with Christian vocabulary.
46. *Wars*, 3.10.20.
47. *Wars*, 3.11.30–31.
48. Called *Massagetai* by Procopius (*Wars*, 3.12.8.), borrowing the label from Herodotus (1.201). The practice of applying classical names to contemporary tribes and countries was one of the conventions of the "secular historians," but Procopius did not aim at consistency; in the first two books of the *Wars*, for instance, the Huns are labeled simply "Huns," or in the case of the "White Huns," sometimes *Ephthalitai*. In the *Vandal War,* Procopius adds the explanatory note that "they now call" the Massagetae "Huns" (*Wars*, 3.11.9.), presumably so that his hypothetical readers from the classical past would not misunderstand.
49. *Wars*, 3.14.17. An "unencumbered man" could travel 210 stades or about 24 English miles in a day: cf. *Wars*, 3.1.17.
50. This was a meeting of Belisarius' *consilium* or advisory council, to which Procopius belonged in his capacity as *assessor*. The description of the meeting is stylized to give Belisarius a "scene" where he can set forth his strategy.

51. Cf. Thucydides, 6.47–49.

52. Cf. the speech of Belisarius to his troops (*Wars,* 3.16.2–8), where he emphasizes the strategic value of maintaining the good will of the Libyans.

53. *Wars,* 3.20.19.

54. *Wars,* 4.7.20–8.1.

55. *Wars,* 4.8.18–23.

56. *Wars,* 4.10.13–25. This passage of Procopius provides the latest evidence we have for the survival of Punic (Phoenician) in North Africa. For an examination of the evidence, see Fergus Millar, "Local Cultures in the Roman Empire: Libyan, Punic and Latin in Roman Africa," *JRS,* vol. 58 (1968), pp. 126–34.

57. Cf. *Wars,* 4.14.39.

58. *Wars,* 4.19.4.

59. *Wars,* 4.22.2.

60. *Wars,* 4.28.52.

61. *Wars,* 8.17.20–22.

62. *Wars,* 5.1.26–29.

63. *Wars,* 5.20.5–20.

64. *Wars,* 5.1.32–39. Symmachus, who suffered execution along with Boethius, is also mentioned.

65. *Wars,* 8.22.7–16.

66. *Wars,* 5.15.11–14.

67. *Wars,* 8.22.5.

68. *Wars,* 5.4.4.

69. *Wars,* 5.5.8–9.

70. This practice was borrowed from Thucydides, but with a change which reflected the progress in military science. Thucydides calculated by the years of the war, which he subdivided into winter and summer seasons, for the summer season was the period of active campaigning, and the winter was relatively idle. For Thucydides' practice, see J. H. Finley, *Thucydides* (Cambridge, Mass., 1942; repr. Ann Arbor, Mich., 1963), pp. 107–8.

71. Cf. J. Haury, *Procopiana* (Augsburg, 1890–91), pp. 8–9.

72. *Wars,* 5.26.19.

73. *Wars,* 5.24.2–3.

74. *Wars,* 5.27.27–28.

75. *Wars,* 5.28.1–50.

76. *Wars,* 6.8.1–18.

77. *Wars,* 6.11.20–22.

78. *Wars,* 6.21.39.

79. *Wars,* 6.22.4.

80. *Wars,* 6.29.1–4.

81. *Wars,* 7.1.4–21.

82. *Wars,* 7.35.1. Knud Hannestad ("Les Forces Militaires d'après la Guerre Gothique de Procope," *Classica et Mediaevalia,* vol. 21 [1960], pp. 136–83) from an examination of the statistics in Procopius, on the numbers of the Gothic and Byzantine forces, attempts to document a change in Procopius' attitude to Belisarius after 540. During the years 536–40, he exaggerated the size of the Gothic army and the losses it suffered, while after 540, he indicates that the Gothic army was about equal in size to its Byzantine counterpart and was greatly its superior in discipline.

83. *Wars,* 7.30.25. Belisarius remained in retirement until 559, when Justinian mustered him out to save Constantinople from an invasion of Kotrigur Huns.

84. *Wars,* 7.36.4–6, 7.35.11, and 8.26.7.

85. Cf. *Wars,* 7.8.1.

86. *Wars,* 7.21.1–11.

87. Cf. John L. Teall, "The Barbarians in Justinian's Armies," *Speculum,* vol. 40 (1965), pp. 294–322.

88. *Wars,* 8.23.42.

89. *Wars,* 8.26.14–17.

90. *Wars,* 8.26.7–10.

91. *Wars,* 8.30.1–20.

Chapter Three

1. For an appreciation of the value of the *Buildings,* see G. Downey, "Justinian as a Builder," *Art Bulletin,* vol. 32 (1950), pp. 262–66.

2. *Bldgs.* 1.3.1.

3. G. Downey, "Notes on Procopius, *De Aedificiis* Book 1," *Studies Presented to David M. Robinson,* vol. 2, (St. Louis, 1953), pp. 719–25; *Constantinople in the Age of Justinian* (Norman, Okla., 1960), pp. 156–59.

4. The accuracy of Procopius' information is emphasized again in a recent study by P. A. MacKay, "Procopius' *De Aedificiis* and the topography of Thermopylae," *AJA,* vol. 67 (1963), pp. 241–55. Mac-Kay points out that Procopius' information in the *Buildings* on the topography of Thermopylae in Greece is better than that which he had included earlier in the *Wars* (2.4.10).

5. *De Magistratibus,* 3.28.4–5. For a translation of this work and a brief account of John's career, see T. F. Carney (trans.), *John the Lydian, On the Magistracies* (Sydney, Australia, 1965).

6. G. Downey, "The Composition of Procopius' *De Aedificiis,*" *TAPA,* vol. 78 (1947), pp. 171–83.

7. *Bldgs.* 2.11.1 and 2.11.8.

8. *Bldgs.* 4.4; 4.11; 5.9.

9. *Bldgs.* 1.1.15. Procopius says that if one examined the reign of Justinian, he would conclude that the rule of Cyrus was child's play (*paidia*). The Greek word for "education" was *paideia,* and hence the *Cyropaedeia* was "The Education of Cyrus."

10. *Bldgs.* 1.1.6: 1.1.12.

11. *Bldgs.* 2.4.21.

12. *Bldgs.* 5.1.3.

13. As suggested by Downey, *op. cit., TAPA,* vol. 78 (1947), pp. 172–73.

14. *Bldgs.* 6.7.18.

15. *Bldgs.* 2.4.1–5.

16. *Bldgs.* 5.4.16; 5.5.19; 1.1.71.

17. *Bldgs.* 1.1.12. "However, the majority of the emperor's achievements have been described by me in my other writings. . . ." This was intended to suggest delicately that the *Wars* had been written in Justinian' honor (see note 10, this chapter), but there is the possibility of a double meaning. See J. Haury, "Prokop und der Kaiser Justinian," *ByzZeit* vol. 37 (1937), pp. 1–9, esp. p. 5.

18. *Bldgs.* 1.2.10. Cf. K. Gantar, "Kaiser Justinian jenem Herbststerngleich. Bemerkung zu Prokops *Aed.* I, 20, 10," *Museum Helveticum,* vol. 19 (1962), pp. 194–96.

19. Cf. 1.11.17; 5.3.18.

20. Eusebius, *De Laudibus Constantini,* 1. 6.

21. There is an extensive literature on the Byzantine concept of kingship and its dependence on Hellenistic political thought, which is now best reviewed in Francis Dvornik, *Early Christian and Byzantine Political Philosophy, Origins and Background, Dumbarton Oaks Studies,* 9 (Washington, D.C., 1966). The importance of Eusebius in the development of the conceptual framework of Byzantine kingship was first recognized by Norman Baynes, "Eusebius and the Christian Empire," *Annuaire de l'Institut d'Histoire Orientale,* vol. 2 (1933–34), pp. 13–18.

22. *Nov.* 105.4. It should be remembered that, while the Hellenistic world accepted divine kingship, the Roman principate had been established by the emperor Augustus within the conceptual framework of the Roman republican constitution, which he claimed to have restored. This "republican concept" of the emperor held that he was not above the law, but was bound to respect it (cf. S. I. Oost, "Galla Placidia and the Law," *Classical Philology,* vol. 53 (1968), p. 120). Hence Roman law long resisted the idea of the divine right of kings, and not until Justinian, is an emperor recognized as "incarnate law," and there-

fore as the source of all laws—a point well made by G. Bagnani, "Divine Right and Roman Law," *Phoenix,* vol. 3 (1949), pp. 51–59. As a student of Roman law, trained before Justinian's legal reforms went into effect, Procopius must have had a somewhat ambiguous concept of the imperial position: from one viewpoint, the strictly legal one, the emperor's authority rested on the law, but in Justinian's own view, which was reflected in his legal reforms, it rested on divine right.

23. Deno J. Geanakoplos ("Church and State in the Byzantine Empire: A Reconsideration of the Problem of Caesaropapism," *Church History,* vol. 34 [1965], pp. 381–403) reminds us that such terms as "sacerdotal kingship" and "caesaropapism" overstate the actual position of the Byzantine emperor, who was always a layman. However, Justinian did call himself "king and priest" (*rex et sacerdos*).

24. *Bldgs.* 1.1.67.

25. *Bldgs.* 1.1.71 and 1.1.76–77.

26. *Bldgs.* 1.1.78.

27. *Bldgs.* 2.2.1–21.

28. *Bldgs.* 2.3.2–14.

29. *Bldgs.* 3.6.12; 5.7.16; 6.2.16–20; 6.2.1–2; 6.5.6.

Chapter Four

1. As was pointed out by J. B. Bury, *A History of the Later Roman Empire from Arcadius to Irene (395 A.D. to 800 A.D.)* (London, 1889), vol. 1, p. 363.

2. *SH,* 1.1–2.

3. *SH,* 30.12–14. However, here Procopius is referring to the imperial intelligence agents who furnished information about Persia.

4. J. B. Bury, *History of the Later Roman Empire from the death of Theodosius I to the death of Justinian* (London, 1923), vol. 2, pp. 426–27.

5. *Bldgs.* 1.11.9.

6. Cf. C. Diehl, *Théodora, Impératrice de Byzance* (Paris, 1904), pp. 5–68. For a more skeptical view, see C. E. Mallett, "The Empress Theodora," *English Historical Review,* vol. 2 (1887), pp. 1–20.

7. C. Diehl, *op. cit.,* pp. 113–22.

8. *SH,* 17.5–6.

9. *SH,* 9.51; *Cod. Justinianus* 5.4.23.5–6.

10. *SH,* 16.2–5; and *Wars,* 5.4.12–31.

11. Cassiodorus, *Variae,* 10.20. Gibbon (*Decline and Fall,* Bury ed. [New York, Heritage Press, 1946], p. 1327, cap. 41, n. 45) accepted this letter as proof of the *Secret History's* tale; however, this is im-

possible. But the fact that Theodora did carry on negotiations of some sort with Gudelina could have given rise to malevolent rumors, reported by Procopius as fact. Cf. T. Hodgkin, *The Letters of Cassiodorus*, (London, 1886), p. 433, n. 1.

12. *SH*, 1.14.

13. *SH*, 1.27.

14. *Wars*, 5.14.4; 5.25.13.

15. P. Bonfante, "Il movente della Storia arcana di Procopio," *Rendiconti dell'Academia Nazionale dei Lincei. Classe di Scienza*, 1932, pp. 381–85.

16. Cf. *Wars*, 1.3.6.

17. B. Rubin, *Das Zeitalter Iustinians* (Berlin, 1960), p. 225.

18. *SH*, 4.15.

19. *SH*, 3.2; cf. 1.26 and 2.2.

20. *SH*, 4.40. The incident, described in *SH*, 4.13–31, is a good example of Antonina's influence at court by virtue of her friendship with Theodora.

21. *Wars*, 6.8.1 and *SH*, 1.28–30.

22. *SH*, 5.14. John's uncle, Vitalian, an able commander, probably of barbarian origin, had led a revolt against Anastasius in 514, with anti-Monophysite support. Defeated but by no means annihilated, he was called to the capital by Justin I, heaped with honors, and then murdered at Justinian's instigation in 520 (cf. *SH*, 6.28). His nephew John was probably always to some extent under suspicion, even before his marriage into Germanus' family, which Theodora regarded as rival candidates for the throne. Procopius clearly admired John, in spite of his enmity with Belisarius, for he inserts a brief eulogy of him into the *Wars* (6.10.10).

23. *Wars*, 7.12.16, reports the enmity between Belisarius and Herodian as a rumor: cf. *SH*, 5.5–7. We last hear of Herodian as one of the officers in charge of Totila's treasure! (*Wars*, 8.34.19). He clearly became a trusted soldier in the Gothic army.

24. *SH*, 5.33: cf. *Wars* 4.22.2.

25. *Wars*, 7.32.9.

26. *SH*, 10.15. He also suggests that there was a certain amount of sham to their differences in theology (*SH*, 10.14).

27. *Wars*, 8.13.14.

28. *SH*, 15.18. Also, the imperial couple did not employ good men because they grew uncomfortable in their presence (*SH*, 22.35).

29. *Wars*, 2.2.6.

30. Cf. *SH*, 6.19–21; 7.39; 8.24; 9.1–2; 13.21–23.

31. Cf. the speech of Sandil, king of the Utrigurs, *Wars*, 8.19.9–22.

32. *Wars,* 8.15.14–19.

33. Procopius accuses Justinian of being responsible for the breach of the "Endless Peace" with Persia (*SH,* 11.12). In the *Wars* Procopius had described the cause which Chosroes alleged for his attack, but with the caveat that he could not say whether Chosroes was speaking the truth or not (*Wars,* 2.1.8–15).

34. *SH,* 19.10; 19.13–15.

35. *SH,* 30.32–33.

36. Cf. C. D. Gordon, "Procopius and Justinian's Financial Policies," *Phoenix,* vol. 13 (1959), pp. 23–30; also C. D. Gordon, "Subsidies in Roman Imperial Defence," *Phoenix,* vol. 3 (1949), pp. 60–69.

37. *SH,* 11.40.

38. *SH,* 29.19. On this legal change, see A. H. M. Jones, *The Greek City from Alexander to Justinian* (Oxford, 1940), p. 250.

39. *SH,* 12.12–13.

40. *SH,* 26.3–4.

41. *SH,* 15.12; cf. 30.27–31.

42. *SH,* 23.8.

43. *SH,* 19.6.

44. He is particularly critical of changes in administrative and legal procedure, which must have affected him and his fellow bureaucrats in a very personal way; e.g., *SH,* 14.4, describing how he reduced the functions of the confidential secretaries (*a secretis*) and 26.2, describing how Justinian downgraded the professional advocates or *rhetores* by making it possible for people to litigate directly under oath in the courts, without the intervention of lawyers. This reform must have made justice cheaper and therefore more attainable by the masses; however, Procopius, himself a *rhetor,* saw it only from the viewpoint of the profession which had suffered a loss of income as a result.

45. *Wars,* 1.24.16.

46. *SH,* 20.17. Junilus' native tongue was Latin, for he came from Libya; cf. 14.3, where Procopius remarks disdainfully on Justinian's mastery of Greek.

47. *SH,* 10.2–3; 9.30.

48. *SH,* 17.7–11.

49. *SH,* 9.16; 9.20–22.

50. *SH,* 17.24.

51. *SH,* 23.20–21.

52. *SH,* 30.18–20.

53. The phrase is taken from Daniel Lerner, "Communication and the Prospects of Innovative Development," in *Communication and*

Change in the Developing Countries (Honolulu, 1967), p. 308. Lerner's remarks (pp. 305–17) are valuable as an examination of traditionalist attitudes in a rapidly changing environment.

54. This aspect is carefully examined by B. Rubin. *Das Zeitalter Iustinians* (Berlin, 1960), pp. 203–17; 440, 454.

55. *SH*, 6.5–9.

56. *SH*, 12.18–19.

57. *SH*, 12.20–22. Cf. K. Gantar, "Kaiser Justinian als Köpfloser Dämon," *ByzZeit*. vol. 54 (1961), pp. 1–3, where the author tries to show that Procopius' demonology is derived from the apocryphal *Testament of Solomon* (cf. C. C. McCown, *The Testament of Solomon*, Leipzig, 1922) and that the headless demon stands for slaughter.

58. *SH*, 12.24–26.

59. *SH*, 12.27.

60. *SH*, 8.13.

61. *SH*, 12.31–32.

62. *SH*, 12.28.

63. *SH*, 12.14–17.

64. *SH*, 18.36–37.

65. Cf. *Bldgs.* 2.6.6, where Procopius speaks of Justinian being entrusted by God with a mission "to watch over the whole empire, and restore it, so far as was possible." This is not the only instance where the *Secret History* carefully contradicts the *Buildings*. In *SH* 22.35, Procopius says that the imperial pair never employed good men; in *Bldgs.* 1.1.26, he marvels at the discernment of the emperor, who always selected the best men for his enterprises.

Chapter Five

1. *Wars*, 3.12.3.

2. Cf. *Wars*, 4.10.25.

3. *Wars*, 8.22.7–16.

4. *Wars*, 3.2.24.

5. *I.e.*, sprung from the earth, and therefore not immigrants from anywhere.

6. *Wars*, 4.10.24–25.

7. *Wars*, 5.15.4–9.

8. *Wars*, 5.23.16–17.

9. Gladiatorial shows had been abolished in the West by the emperor Honorius, but wild-beast fights and the baiting of wild animals continued down to Procopius' own day. Procopius' disdain is explicit; cf. C. Jenkins, "Procopiana," *JRS*, vol. 37 (1947), 74–81.

10. *Bldgs.* 6.4.5.

11. *Bldgs.* 4.3.12.
12. *Bldgs.* 4.2.8–9.
13. Cf. J. H. Finley, *Thucydides* (Cambridge, Mass., 1942), pp. 82–88.
14. *Wars,* 1.1.6–17.
15. *Wars,* 8.6.9.
16. *Wars,* 3.8.27.
17. *Wars,* 5.27.27–29.
18. *Wars,* 2.29.33–43.
19. *Wars,* 7.13.14.
20. Cf. *Wars,* 5.3.5–9. He dismisses as foolish the attempt to define the nature of God.
21. *Wars,* 4.14.12–15.
22. *Wars,* 6.10.10.
23. *Wars,* 7.17.10.
24. *Wars,* 8.11.39–54.
25. *Wars,* 8.14.
26. *Wars,* 4.16.12–16.
27. G. Downey, "The Persian Campaign in Syria in A.D. 540," *Speculum,* vol. 28 (1953), pp. 340–48.
28. *Wars,* 2.6.14–15.
29. *Wars,* 7.39.11.
30. *Wars,* 7.40.9.
31. *SH,* 5.8–11.
32. *Wars,* 2.10.4–5.
33. *Wars,* 7.13.17. The whole of *Wars,* 7.13.15–19, is important for Procopius' assessment of the Gothic War after 540. God, he says, had determined to assist Totila and the Goths, and the best of Belisarius' plans failed to turn out well.
34. *Wars,* 7.1.23–33.
35. *Wars,* 7.36.4–6. The other business was the controversy centering around the "Edict of the Three Chapters," the prime mover of which had been the crypto-Monophysite bishop of Procopius' native city, Theodore Askidas.
36. *Wars,* 8.26.7.
37. E. Stein (*Histoire du Bas-Empire,* vol 2 [Paris-Bruxelles-Amsterdam, 1949], p. 715), speaks of Procopius' boundless skepticism and of his wavering from rationalist fatalism to a theism vaguely Christian and to superstitious credulity.
38. *The Divine Institutes,* 8.16, from *The Works of Lactantius,* trans. W. Fletcher, in *The Ante-Nicene Christian Library,* vol. 1 (Edinburgh, 1871), pp. 465–66.
39. H. St. L. B. Moss (*Cambridge Mediaeval History,* vol. 4, pt. I

[Cambridge, 1966], p. 12) notes that the Cynic freedom of speech was inherited by the monks in the Byzantine Empire.

Chapter Six

1. See J. B. Bury, *A History of the Later Roman Empire from Arcadius to Irene* (London, 1889), p. 179 ("at core a pagan"); F. Dahn, *Prokopius von Caesarea* (Berlin, 1865) pp. 181–82, 217 (mixture of Christian and theist, a fatalist); B. Rubin, *RE*, Bd. 23. 1. cols 331–32 (skeptic); E. Stein, *op. cit.*, p. 715 (skeptic, fatalist, theist, superstitious); G. Downey, "Paganism and Christianity in Procopius," *Church History*, vol. 18 (1949), pp. 89–102 (generally Christian, with parallels in his thought to Saint Augustine); Averil Cameron, "The 'Skepticism' of Procopius," *Historia*, vol. 15 (1966), pp. 466–82 (generally a conventional Christian, but one who had not thought out all the implications of combining classical historiography and the Christian outlook).

2. See H. Nicholson, *Monarchy* (London, 1962), p. 109 (a Jew); B. Rubin, "Das Römische Reich im Osten Byzanz," in *Propyläen Weltgeschichte. Eine Universalgeschichte*, ed. G. Mann and A. Heuss (Berlin-Frankfurt-Vienna, 1963), vol. 4, p. 641 (a Syrian or a Jew); R. Atwater, *The Secret History of Procopius*, translated with Introduction (New York, 1927), p. 1 (a Samaritan who conformed to Christianity for political reasons). The possibility that Procopius was a heretic has been put up by P. Bonfante, "Il Movente della Storia Arcana di Procopio," *Rendiconte della Academia Nazionale dei Lincei*, Classe di Scienze Morali (1932), pp. 381–85, following a suggestion of D. Comparetti.

3. *Wars*, 2.12.22–23.

4. *Wars*, 2.9.14; 3.10.18.

5. *Wars*, 5.11.26; 5.14.4.

6. *Wars*, 5.3.6–7.

7. *Wars*, 8.25.13.

8. *SH*, 11.33. For the argument that this is the same promise as that expressed in *Wars*, 8.25.13, see H. B. Dewing, *Procopius*, vol. 6, *The Anecdota or Secret History* ("The Loeb Classical Library," Cambridge, Mass., and London, 1935), pp. 362–64.

9. *SH*, 11.14–33.

10. *Cod. Iustinianus*, 1.15.17; 1.15.18.

11. *SH*, 11.15.

12. *SH*, 11.29–30.

13. *SH*, 13.7.

14. *SH*, 13.4.

15. *SH*, 11.21–23.

16. *SH*, 11.25. The passage implies that these Samaritans who pretended to adopt Christianity were eminently sensible.

17. *SH*, 28.16–19.

18. *Wars*, 5.8.41; 5.10.25.

19. He must have passed for an orthodox Christian, certainly; otherwise he could not have held the post of *assessor* (cf. *Cod. Iustinianus*, 1. 5.12).

20. *Wars*, 1.7.5–11.

21. *Wars*, 2.4.1–3.

22. *Bldgs.* 1.7.6–16.

23. *SH*, 9.28.

24. *SH*, 3.30.

25. *SH*, 1.26; cf. 22.26–28 for Theodora's reputation as a sorceress.

26. 2.22.

27. Cf. P. Pedech, *La Méthode Historique de Polybe* (Paris, 1964), pp. 331–54.

28. Cf. C. N. Cochrane, *Christianity and Classical Culture* (Oxford, 1944), pp. 456–516.

29. *Wars*, 4.6.34.

30. *Wars*, 8.32.28–30.

31. *Wars*, 5.5.18–19.

32. *Wars*, 8.33.24–25.

33. *Wars*, 3.21.7.

34. *Wars*, 1.18.17–23.

35. *Wars*, 2.17.16.

36. *Wars*, 3.18.2.

37. *SH*, 4.44–45.

38. *Wars*, 5.9.30; 5.10.29.

39. *Wars*, 1.24.31.

40. *Wars*, 6.29.32.

41. *Wars*, 7.8.24.

42. *Wars*, 3.19.6.

43. *Wars*, 4.28.12–13.

44. Herodotus, 1.90.

45. *Wars*, 3.2.35.

46. *SH*, 30.34. We must be hesitant in ascribing any systematic theology to Procopius; however, like his contemporaries, he no doubt subscribed to the belief that the Christian empire on earth should be an imitation of heaven, with the emperor acting as vicegerent of God, and since it was obvious to him that this was not the case under Justinian, he inverted the concept and drew upon the prophecies of the Antichrist. The concept of the empire as the imitation of heaven

was first articulated by Eusebius and contrasts with Saint Augustine's view that Christian society on earth is a mixture of two kingdoms, one an earthly city and the other the city of God. Cf. F. E. Cranz, "Kingdom and Polity in Eusebius of Caesarea," *Harvard Theological Review,* vol. 45 (1952), pp. 47–66.

47. 5.3.7–8.

48. *Bldgs.* 4.3.12.

Chapter Seven

1. H. Braun, "Procopius Caesariensis Quatenus Imitatus Sit Thucydidem" (Diss, Inaug. Erlangae, 1865), p. 4.

2. *Wars,* 2.3.32–53.

3. *Wars,* 2.9.1–7.

4. *Wars,* 6.6.14–34.

5. Cf. F. Pringsheim, "The Character of Justinian's Legislation," *Law Quarterly Review,* vol. 56 (1948), pp. 229–46, esp. p. 233.

6. Cf. Krumbacher, *op. cit.,* p. 234.

7. These quotations are taken from W. H. Parks, "Some Suggestions derived from a Comparison of the Histories of Thucydides and Procopius," *TAPA,* vol. 24 (1893), pp. xl-xlii.

8. Robert Graves, *Count Belisarius* (New York, 1939).

9. *Procopius: History of the Wars, Secret History* and *Buildings,* newly translated, edited, abridged, and with an introduction by Averil Cameron. "The Great Histories" series. (New York, Washington Square Press, 1967).

Selected Bibliography

PRIMARY SOURCES

1. Procopius of Caesarea, *Opera Omnia* recognovit Jacobus Haury (Leipzig, "Teubner Library of Greek and Roman Writers," 3 vols., 1905–13; reprinted in 4 vols., 1962–64.) This is now the standard text of Procopius' three works, the *History of the Wars of Justinian;* the *Secret History* (*Anekdota*); and the *Buildings* (*Peri Ktismaton*), replacing Dindorf's earlier unsatisfactory text in the series, *Scriptores Historiae Byzantinae* (3 vols., Bonn, 1833–38).

2. *La Guerra Gotica di Procopio di Cesarea. Testo greco emendato sui manoscritti con traduzione italiana,* by Domenico Comparetti. 3 vols. Rome, Istituto Storico Italiano, 1895, 1896, 1898. A new edition of the Gothic War, with a translation into Italian. Comparetti improved greatly on the Greek text of Dindorf by adopting readings from the thirteenth-century Codex Vaticanus, which Dindorf had neglected.

3. Procopius, with an English translation by H. B. Dewing, 6 vols. The Loeb Classical Library. Vol. 1, "The Persian War" (Books I and II), London, Heinemann; New York: Macmillan, 1914. Vol. 2, "The Vandalic War" (Books III and IV), London, Heinemann; New York, Putnam. Vols. 3–5, "The Gothic War" (Books, V, VI, VII, and VIII), London, Heinemann; New York, Putnam, 1919, 1924, 1928. Vol. 6, "The Anecdota or Secret History," London, Heinemann; Cambridge, Mass.: Harvard University Press, 1935. Vol. 7, "The Buildings" (with the collaboration of Glanville Downey), London, Heinemann; Cambridge, Mass.: Harvard University Press, 1935.
This edition follows the general format of the Loeb Classical Library, with the Greek text and English translation on opposite pages. The text is that of Haury, with some modifications in the last volume.

4. *Le Inedite: libro nono delle istorie di Procopio di Cesarea, testo*

greco emendato sui manoscritti con traduzione italiana a cura di Domenico Comparetti, edited and published after Comparetti's death by Domenico Bassi. Fonti per la Storia d'Italia, no. 61. Rome, Istituto Storico Italiano, 1928.

In this posthumous edition of the *Secret History,* Comparetti put forward the view that the work was written late in the author's life, in 558–59, after he had retired to his native city, Caesarea, and that it articulated popular resentment in Palestine against Justinian.

5. Procopius, *Secret History,* translated by Richard Atwater, with a forward by Arthur E. R. Boak. Ann Arbor, Mich.: University of Michigan Press, 1961. A reprint of the translation by Richard Atwater (New York, 1927) with a new, useful introduction, replacing Atwater's idiosyncratic preface in the original edition. Available now as a paperback, Ann Arbor series, AA80.

6. Procopius, *The Secret History,* translated with an introduction by G. A. Williamson. Harmondsworth, England: Penguin Books, 1966. A new translation for the Penguin Classics series, with a good, useful introduction.

7. Procopius, *History of the Wars, Secret History and Buildings,* translated, edited, and abridged, with an introduction by Averil Cameron. The Great Histories series. New York: Washington Square Press (W.1406), 1967. This new translation abridges heavily in order to fit into the format of the series. *The Buildings* is represented only by a few selections from the first book. However, the *Wars* is dealt with more generously, and brief summaries fill in the omitted portions.

SECONDARY SOURCES

BURY, J. B. *A History of the Later Roman Empire from Arcadius to Irene, (395 A.D. to 800 A.D.),* 2 vols. London and New York: Macmillan. Volume 2, pp. 359–64, contains a useful essay on Procopius, where Bury argues against the authenticity of the *Secret History.* However, he later changed his mind, and much of what he says here is superseded by the next entry.

————. *A History of the Later Roman Empire from the Death of Thedosius I to the Death of Justinian, (395 A.D.–565),* 2 vols. London: Macmillan, 1923; reprinted, New York: Dover Books, 1958. Bury's later, more authoritative treatment of the period devotes a brief section (pp. 417–30) to Procopius.

CAMERON, A. and A. "Christianity and Tradition in the Historiography of the Late Empire," *Classical Quarterly,* vol. 14 [n.s.], (1964), pp. 316–28. A study of the literary peculiarities of the "secular historians."

CAMERON, AVERIL. "The 'Skepticism' of Procopius," *Historia,* vol. 15, (1966), pp. 466–82. An important study of Procopius' so-called pagan outlook, which arrives at the conclusion that Procopius was a conventional Christian.

————, *Agathias,* Cambridge: Cambridge University Press, 1970. A. study of Procopius' continuator, which contains an important section on Christian history in the classical manner, applicable to Procopius as well as Agathias. This book, unfortunately, reached me too late to use.

DAHN, FELIX. *Procopius von Caesarea. Ein Beitrag zur Historiographie der Völkerwanderung und des Sinkenden Römerthums.* Berlin: Mittler, 1865. An important pioneering study. His comments on Procopius' aristocratic outlook are still very valuable.

DEWING, H. B. "The secret history of Procopius of Caesarea." *TAPA,* vol. 62 (1931), pp. xl-xli. A very brief summary of the case for the authenticity of the *Secret History.*

DIEHL, C. *Justinien et la civilisation byzantine au VIᵉ siècle.* Paris: E. Leroux, 1901. A lively account of Justinian which puts its main emphasis on the art of the period. However, pp. xii-xx give a brief appreciation of Procopius.

————. *Théodora, impératrice de Byzance.* Paris: H. Piazza, 1904, 3rd ed. A semipopular account of Theodora with a good appreciation of the value of the *Secret History* as a source for the empress' early life.

DOWNEY, G. "Paganism and Christianity in Procopius." *Church History,* vol. 18 (1949), pp. 89–102. Downey dissented from the view that Procopius was half-pagan and concluded that he was a Christian of independent and skeptical mind.

————. "The Persian Campaign in Syria in A.D. 540." *Speculum,* vol. 28 (1953), pp. 340–48. A study of the sack of Antioch by Chosroes, which arrives at the conclusion that Procopius was unduly biased in favor of Germanus in his account.

ELFERINK, M. A. "TYXH et Dieu chez Procope de Césarée." *Acta Classica,* vol. 10 (1967), pp. 111–34. Elferink examines Procopius' concept of chance and concludes that the underlying theme of his *Wars* is the opposition of a rational God and irrational contingency.

EVANS, J. A. S. "The Dates of the *Anecdota* and the *De Aedificiis* of Procopius." *Classical Philology,* vol. 64 (1969), pp. 29–30. Advances the view that the *Secret History* and the *Buildings* were written at the same time, between 558 and 560.

————. "Procopius and the Emperor Justinian." *The Canadian Historical Association. Historical Papers,* 1968, pp. 126–39. An attempt to document the manner in which Procopius' outlook changed between 527 and 560.

GORDON, C. D. "Procopius and Justinian's Financial Policies." *Phoenix*, vol. 13 (1959), pp. 23–30. An excellent study which attempts to put into perspective the charges in the *Secret History* that Justinian was wilfully extravagant.

GOUGH, MICHAEL. *The Early Christians.* London: Thames and Hudosn, 1961. Ancient Peoples and Places Series, vol. 19. Contains a succinct study of the art and architecture of Justinian's reign (pp. 187–206).

HANNESTAD, K. "Les Forces Militaires d'après la Guerre gothique de Procope." *Classica et Mediaevalia*, vol. 21 (1960), pp. 136–83. A study of Procopius' statistics in the *Gothic War* which concludes that he persistently exaggerated the size of the Gothic army before 540, whereas after that date, his enthusiasm for Belisarius cooled, and he presented his figures more objectively.

HAURY J. *Procopiana.* Program des Königlichen Realgymnasium für das Studienjahr 1890/91. Augsburg: Haas and Grabherr. An important study which argued for the first time that the *Secret History* should be dated to 550, on the basis of internal evidence.

KUMANIECKI, K. "Zu Prokops Anecdota." *ByzZeit*, vol. 27 (1927) pp. 19–21. An argument for the authenticity of the *Secret History* based on an examination of the metrical *clausulae*.

RUBIN, B. "Prokopios von Kaisareia." *Paulys Realencyclopädie der Classischen Altertumwissenschaft*, Bd. 23.1. Stuttgart: Alfred Druckenmuller, 1957, cols. 273–599. This long article (the text appeared three years earlier as a separate book) is the most substantial study of Procopius to date.

————. *Das Zeitalter Iustinians*, vols. 1– . Berlin: Walter de Gruyter, 1960. A multivolume work still in progress. The first volume contains an excellent study of Procopius' works (pp. 173–226) which supplements the same author's earlier work on Procopius (n. 16).

————. "Der Fürst der Damonen. Ein Beitrag zur Interpretation von Prokops Anekdota." *ByzZeit*, vol. 44 (1951), pp. 468–81. A study of the Antichrist concepts in the *Secret History*, which concludes that they are derived from the intellectual world of early Christianity.

STEIN, E. *Histoire du Bas-Empire.* Vol. 2, *De la disparition de l'Empire d'Occident à la mort de Justinien, (476-565).* Paris-Bruxelles-Amsterdam: Desclée de Brouwer, 1949. The second volume of a major work on the late empire by a great German scholar, edited and issued posthumously by J.-R. Palanque. Contains a brief section on Procopius (pp. 709–23) and also an attempt to redate the *Buildings* to 555. (Excursus V, p. 837.)

TEUFFEL, W. S. *Studien und charakteristiken zur Griechischen und Römischen sowie zur Deutschen Literaturgeschichte.* Leipzig: B. G. Teubner, 1871, pp. 191–236. Teuffel's chapter on Procopius is still one of the most valuable studies on the subject.

URE, P. N. *Justinian and His Age.* Harmondsworth: England; and Baltimore: Penguin, 1951. A good, succinct book on Justinian which relies heavily on Procopius and his continuator, Agathias; contains a good appreciation of them both.

VEH, OTTO. *Zur Geschichtsschreibung und Weltauffassung des Prokop von Caesarea.* Wissenschaftliche Beitrage . . . des Gymnasiums Bayreuth, Part 1, 1950/51; Part 2, 1951/52; Part 3 (pp. 3–17), 1952/53. A good, relatively brief study of Procopius, which covers all his works.

Index

⫯3597

DATE DUE

GAYLORD			PRINTED IN U.S.A.